INDIAN INSTANT POT COOKBOOK:

Healthy and Easy Indian Instant Pot Pressure Cooker Recipes.

Henry Wilson

Copyright © [Henry Wilson]

All rights reserved. No part of this guide may be reproduced in any form without permission in writing from the publisher except in the case of brief quotations embodied in critical articles or reviews.

CONTENTS

Introduction 6
Indian Cuisine 7
    North Indian Food 7
    South Indian Food 8
What Food and Spices are Mainly Used in Indian Cuisine? 9
    Using Indian spices 9
Indian Recipes for Instant Pot/Pressure Cooker 12
Chicken – Indian Style 13
    Butter Chicken 13
    Instant Pot Chicken Masala 14
    Chicken Chettinad 15
    Mughlai Zaafrani Chicken 16
    Chicken Curry with Coconut Milk 18
    Chicken Tikka Masala 19
    Chicken Biryani 20
    Asian Chicken and Rice 22
    Indian Butter Chicken 23
Meat – Indian Style 25
    Instant Pot Beef Fry Kerala Style 25
    Goan Pork Instant Pot Vindaloo 26
    Instant Pot Gosht 27
    Instant Pot/Pressure Cooker Mutton Korma 28
    Spicy Beef Curry Slow Cooking 30
    Lamb Curry 31
Indian Fish Curry Recipes 33
    Indian Fish Curry 33
    Instant Pot Fish Tikka 34
    Coconut Milk Fish Curry 35
    Instant Pot Fish Coconut Curry 36
    Fish Molee 37
    Indian Coconut Shrimp Curry 38

    Pressure Cooked Coconut Fish Curry 39

Rice Indian Recipes 41

    Chicken Biriyani 41

    Jeera Rice 42

    Ghee Rice 43

    Lemon Rice 44

    South Indian Curd Rice 44

    Indian Lemon Rice 46

Beans Recipes 47

    Beans Thoran 47

    Spicy Green Beans 47

    Beans Patoli Curry 48

    Cluster Beans Fry 49

    Green Beans with Potatoes 50

Dal Recipes 52

    Guajarati Dal 52

    Instant Pot Daal Tadka 53

    Daal Makhani 54

    Panjabi Dal Tadka 55

    Instant Pot Dal Fry 56

Vegetable Recipes 58

    South Indian Sambar 58

    Avial (Mixed Vegetable) Curry 59

    Kadai Mushroom Curry 60

    Navaratan Korma 61

    Vegetable Korma 64

    Cauliflower and Potato Stir Fry 66

    Egg Curry 67

    Butter Chickpeas 68

    Vegetable Biryani 69

    Vegetable Korma 70

    Spiced Potato and Eggplant 72

    Langar Dal 72

    Egg Biryani 73

Indian Desserts **75**

    Gulab Jamun 75

    Instant Pot Gajar Halwa 76

    Sweet Pongal 76

    Kaju Barfi 77

    Paal Payasam (South Indian Dessert in Milk) 78

Soup Recipes **80**

    Tomato Soup 80

    Beetroot Carrot Ginger Soup 81

    Mutton Shorba 82

    Instant Pot Lentil Soup 83

    Curried Chicken Soup 84

Keto Indian Recipes **86**

    Keto Mutton Masala 86

    Keto Instant Pot Paneer Bhurji 87

    Spiced Mustard Greens 88

    Keto Indian Lamb Curry 89

    Keto Indian Butter Chicken 91

Conclusion **93**

INTRODUCTION

People say money is life, but in reality, life is about scrumptious good food. Good food means a good life, and by good food, we mean healthy, luxurious and delicious Indian cuisine. Eternally delicious food involving tasty Indian spices equals incredible and appetizing dishes.

No other cuisine comes up with a wide variety of flavors like sour, sweet, spicy and hot all the same time. One of the main spices which are used in almost every dish of Indian cuisine is 'Garam Masala.' The best Dal (lentil) and vegetarian recipes use garam masala as the main spice to make it flavorful. Indian recipes have the best enviable flavors, and this is often due to the spices used to make the dishes.

India is one of those countries which have a wide variety of dishes to try and experience different flavors in all of them. This book has all the best Indian dishes which are luscious and delectable. Even non-vegetarians will find this book useful because it contains chicken, meat and Indian fish recipes.

Why should vegetarians have all the mouth-watering and succulent food? Foodies must grab this book, because it has everything you need for a palatable Indian dish. The book contains the best Indian recipes which will make you want to try them right now. Enjoy the widest variety of savory food with the best flavors of Indian spices and ingredients.

INDIAN CUISINE

India, the land of spices has a unique place in the world of culinary culture. Whenever we think about Indian cuisine, the thoughts of aromatic dishes lavishly treated with spices and herbs stay dominant in the forefront. It has a variety of mouth-watering dishes, peppered in herbs and spices, that are considered as gourmet meals all over the world.

The Dravidian and Aryan civilization has influenced Indian recipes. A lot of factors influence the Indian culinary culture and the hot weather in India is the greatest among them, enabling some of the spices and ingredients to grow.

Being a large country with different culture, faiths, and lifestyles, you can find different styles of cuisines in India. Each of these cuisines maintains its uniqueness which stands as its cultural identity.

Let us now discuss the two major divisions namely North Indian and South Indian food.

NORTH INDIAN FOOD

Northern India is known for its extreme type of climate and rainfall. Cooking style differs from each state, and the choice of herbs and spices are also very distinct. India has a significant subdivision in food like vegetarian and non-vegetarian types.

Kashmiri Food: Kashmiri dishes have a long-lasting impact of Persian, Afghanistan and Central Asian culinary styles. The culinary knowledge of Kashmiri pundits profoundly influences it. A lot of dried fruits and poppy seeds find their way into every dish you'll find there.

Mughlai Food: Since the Mughals invaded and ruled India, the country has adapted its style of having non-vegetarian dishes. Use of 'garam masala,' kewra water, and other spices are prominent in their culinary form.

Punjabi Food: There are a large variety of dishes in the culinary culture of Punjab which satiates the vegetarian as well as non-vegetarian taste buds. The use of freshly harvested sag leaves, herbs, and various lentils are quite evident. Punjabi food is relished all over the country and is readily available in the restaurants.

Gujarati Food: Gujarati food has a collection of typical lip-smacking dishes and is mainly vegetarian. In Gujarati cooking, it adopts a different style of flavors, and you will love the various blends.

Rajasthani Food: Rajasthani food is primarily vegetarian. A Rajasthani thali is well known for its delicious food and blend of spices in its curries and desserts. The usage of ghee is very much prominent here.

Maharashtrian Food: Maharashtra has its own specialty, and you will love the easy to afford and popular street food specialties like Vada-paw and Paw-bhaji. Here, any person will enjoy a filling meal at the most affordable price.

Goan Food: Anybody who loves seafood will find Goa heavenly. Goa specializes in wine and gigantic prawns with a plethora of other seafood. Cooked in authentic spices with a blend of coconut oil, the Goan food stands at a class of its own.

Bengali Food: Bengal is famous for its fish dishes. Various sea and river water fishes are available and are a regular component in every household. The usage of Panchforon (five spices) and mouthwatering sweet dishes are amongst the specialties of Bengal.

SOUTH INDIAN FOOD

The majority of South Indian food consists of – dosa, idli, vada, medu vada, rasam, uttapam, sambhar, chutney and boiled rice. Well, there are variations in the states - Andhra Pradesh, Tamilnadu, Telangana, Kerala, and Karnataka.

Karnataka Food: The food of Karnataka is mostly the same as other South Indian states. Some specialty prevails in Coorg and Mysore which are famous for their pork dishes and special dosas. The main accompaniments are the spicy pickles, curries, and buttermilk.

Kerala Food: The specialty of Kerala is the use of coconut in almost every dish. Non-vegetarian dishes have got characteristically rich spices and of course a blend of typical coconut flavor. The Malabar style of cooking will tantalize your taste buds

Tamil Food: If you're fond of vegetarian food, then Tamilnadu must be a heaven for you. The specialties there are idli, dosa, and rasam. Try the Pongal, vada sambhar for a mouth-watering experience. If you like hot and sour, then Tamilnadu food will never fail to impress you.

Telangana Food: Telangana has its own food styles apart from the regular south Indian staple foods. Their specialty is a soup with the ingredient tamarind. You will be amazed by the unique meat dishes which have a blend of all spices, coconut milk, and Kari leaves giving them a rich flavor.

Andhra Pradesh Food: Andhra food stands very close to Telangana food as both states reflect a common culture and their meals are a staple diet for entire Southern India. Enjoy the specialty like tamarind rice, Koora and the various styles of gravy and fries with lentils.

If you travel to Andaman and Nicobar islands, you will find similar sort of dishes which are considered the main food of Southern India. Seafood is popular over there, and they use dried fruits for topping to make the dishes attractive. There are some tribal influence in the local food, and you will enjoy the authentic seafood served with traditional herbs.

India specializes in a diverse range of different styles of food. If you think of biriyani, this differs depending on whether it is done in the Malabar (north Kerala), Lucknow or Hyderabad styles. With vegetarian food, Gujrat and Rajasthan offer a fiercely competitive style. If you want a variety of fish dishes, compare and contrast those from Bengal, Kerala and other eastern states of India.

If you want an easy and affordable breakfast, South Indian dishes have no match. If you're looking for a job or business in the financial capital of the country, satisfy your belly with affordable lip-smacking street food. Indian food has rightly influenced the world for its spicy flavor and incredible rich varieties. You will have a lip-smacking time with some of the best Indian recipes throughout this book.

WHAT FOOD AND SPICES ARE MAINLY USED IN INDIAN CUISINE?

The Indian cuisine is characterized by its subtle and sophisticated use of spices and herbs to transform an otherwise standard recipe instantly. If you ask, I would say that the heart of Indian cuisine lies in the spices used. Any Indian food is incomplete without the unique blend of spice mixture. Indians not only use it to spice up their food, but they also spice up drinks and even sweets with their exquisite spices well known for its wonderful aromatics.

'Masala' is a quite common word used in Indian cuisine which is a Hindi word meaning 'spice.' So, whenever a combination of spices or condiments are mixed it falls under the general category 'masala.' Indian cuisine consists of an extensive range of spices using in both whole and ground form and often combined into a complex spice mixture.

USING INDIAN SPICES

Most of the Indian spices are dry roasted to release their aroma and essential oils contained, before they are ground (some exceptions exist like nutmeg). While some spices can be easily blended using a mortar, it is usually recommended to use a powerful spice blender to make sure that you have a thoroughly ground spice mixture as some spices can be very hard to blend to a powder form.

So here goes the popular Indian spices used in Indian cuisine.

Turmeric:

Turmeric looks similar to ginger root, but it can be identified by its bright orange-yellow color. It is used in Indian dishes for its antibacterial properties and intensive color it gives to dishes. It is mainly used in powder form for the Indian dishes.

Chili powder:

Indian chili powder is the next most common spice after turmeric, which is an essential spice made from spicy ground chilies. You can find different varieties of chilies.

Cardamom:

Cardamom is an incredible aromatic spice with a spicy sweet flavor that enhances sweet and savory dishes. Black and green cardamom are the 2 varieties commonly used in Indian cuisine. Green is the most commonly used variety that is used in lassi, chicken curry, meat dishes, and Indian desserts, etc.

hole green cardamom is used while preparing 'garam masala' (hot spices), or you can also open the pod and use the black seeds. While green cardamom is mild, black cardamom is very powerful. It's mostly just the seeds that are used when using black cardamom, and if it is used as a whole, it is recommended to remove it from the food before serving as it is very spicy and strong.

Cassia Bark:

Cassia bark is an enticing spice, commonly known as Chinese cinnamon and it is similar to cinnamon but a bit different from it. Cassia is easily distinguishable by this rough and tree bark-like texture and known for its milder flavor. Cassia bark can be used in all Indian dishes like vegetable curries and meat varieties.

Cumin Seeds:

Cumin seeds are a commonly used Indian spice in North Indian cuisine and are distinguishable by their distinctive and robust flavor. Cumin seeds should have more aroma while roasting and give a sweet flavor to dishes. It can be use either whole or in powdered form, and it is one of the main ingredients in Indian Garam masala.

Black mustard seeds:

In India, black mustard seeds are more widely used than the large yellow mustard seeds which are very common in western countries. Black mustard seeds have a strong but pleasing flavor and are well known for their digestive qualities. They can be spluttered (fried until they make a hissing nose) in oil and are using for tempering in south Indian dishes. It is an inevitable spluttering ingredient for tempering curries, vegetables and to flavor pickles.

Cloves:

Cloves are a common spice used in Indian dishes that have a medicinal and robust flavor that comes from the essential oils contained in them. Cloves are used either as whole or blended into spice mixtures. Cloves also need to be used in the right quantities as they might overpower other mild spices in a dish.

Asafetida:

Commonly known as Hing, which has a unique place in Indian cuisines. It is prominent for its digestive properties and it enhances flavor in some of Indian dishes. Not all recipes call for Hing, but it is commonly used when cooking beans and lentils, Sambhar and pickles.

Other complementary spices using in Indian dishes are;

- Coriander seeds
- Fenugreek seeds
- Carom seeds
- Fennel seeds
- Nigella seeds
- Nutmeg
- Peppercorns
- Saffron
- Bay leaves

While cooking Indian recipes, spices have to use in the right quantities to get the precise balance of taste. Some spices are extremely hot; hence their use in food should be always be kept to a moderate level. The aroma of the spices increases the flavor and taste of the food. They are healthy because the spices have therapeutic health benefits. Spices are one of the necessary ingredients of Indian recipes, which makes it unique in taste.

Indian Recipes for

Instant Pot/Pressure Cooker

Chicken – Indian Style

Butter Chicken

Preparation: 40 minutes | Cooking: 20 minutes | Servings: 8

Ingredients:

Marinade section:

- Fresh chicken – 1½ pounds
- Fresh ginger paste - ½ teaspoon
- Garlic paste – ½ teaspoon
- Red chili powder – 1 teaspoon
- Curd – 2 cups
- Salt – to taste

Sauce section:

- Fresh butter – 6 ounces
- Pureed tomato – 1 pound
- Black cumin seeds – ½ teaspoon
- Sugar – ½ teaspoon
- Sliced green chilies – 4
- Crushed fenugreek leaves – ½ teaspoon
- Fresh cream – 3½ ounces

Cooking directions:

The first step is to marinate the chicken:

- In a mixing bowl, put red chili powder, ginger and garlic paste, curd and salt.
- Mix thoroughly.
- Now put the chicken pieces into the mix and coat with the marinade.
- Refrigerate the marinated chicken for 6 hours in a closed container.

The next step is to prepare the sauce:

- For the gravy preparation, turn on your Instant Pot in SAUTE mode.
- Add butter, when the display panel shows 'hot.'
- When the butter starts to melt, add tomato puree and sauté till the raw smell goes.
- Add cumin seeds and red chili powder.
- Now add salt as per your taste and mix it well with the butter. The whole process will take about 3-5 minutes.
- After mixing the ingredients with the butter add the chicken pieces, sliced green chilies, and crushed fenugreek leaves. Make sure it has enough liquid for cooking.

- Stop sautéing by pressing the START/STOP button.
- Close the lid and set the Instant Pot to Poultry manual mode and set timer to 5 minutes.
- When the set time elapses, wait for 10 minutes for natural release of the pressure.
- Again change the cooking mode to SAUTÉ and continue cooking for about 5 minutes without closing the lid. Make sure the sauce consistency is okay.
- Add fresh cream to the sauce before serving.
- Serve and enjoy the yummy curry with hot rice or a butter naan.

Nutritional Values:

Calories: 346.20 |Carbs: 5.2g |Fats: 26.2g |Protein: 21.8g | Cholesterol: 116.7 mg | Fiber: 0 g | Sodium: 582.6mg

INSTANT POT CHICKEN MASALA

Preparation: 20 minutes | Cooking: 30 minutes | Servings: 4

Ingredients:

- Chicken pieces with bone – 1½ pounds
- Medium sized onions – 3
- Tomatoes (chopped) – 3
- Green chilies – 2
- Coriander seeds – 2 tsp
- Cumin seeds – 2 tsp
- Black peppercorns – 12
- Dried red chilies – 5
- Ginger garlic paste – 2 tablespoons
- Cashew nut paste – 2 tablespoons
- Oil – 3 tablespoons
- Salt – to taste

Cooking directions:

- Select the Instant Pot SAUTÉ mode on low heat for a minute.
- Pour oil, when the display shows 'hot,' and fry coriander seeds, cumin seeds, and peppercorns for 2-3 minutes.
- Now add dried chilies and roast it for about 1 minute until it releases the fragrance.
- Stop sauté by pressing START/STOP when the fragrance emanates and allow it cool for some time.
- When the heat has settled down, grind the powder coarsely and keep it aside.
- Now put the chopped tomatoes in a blender and puree them.
- Again, keep the setting on SAUTÉ mode on high heat for a minute.
- Pour oil and when the oil becomes hot add finely chopped onions and sauté for about 2 minutes until the onion becomes soft and translucent.
- Now add garlic, green chilies and ginger paste. Stir continuously for a minute.

- Add a little water and continue sautéing for a minute.
- Now add all the ground spices and sauté for half a minute.
- Put the chicken into the mix, stir occasionally and cook for 2-3 minutes.
- Pour the puree over the chicken.
- Stop SAUTÉ mode by pressing START/STOP.
- Close the lid and pressure valve.
- Cook on high pressure for about 5 minutes.
- Let the pressure release naturally.
- Add salt, cashew nut paste, and adequate water and cover the lid.
- Select sauté mode on high heat and cook for about 15 minutes.
- Serve hot with fried rice or plain rice.

Nutritional values:

Calories: 1605 |Carbohydrates: 55.7 grams | Protein: 206.9 grams | Fat: 61.5 grams| Fibers: 18.9 grams

CHICKEN CHETTINAD

Preparation: 15 minutes | Cooking: 30 minutes | Servings: 4

Ingredients:

- Chicken pieces with bone – 1 pound
- Finely chopped large onion – 1
- Finely chopped tomatoes – 2
- Curry leaves – a handful
- Bay leaf – 1
- Oil – 2 tablespoons

To prepare the marinade:

- Turmeric – 1 teaspoon
- Chili powder – ¼ teaspoon
- Curd – 1 tablespoon
- Fresh ginger paste – 1 teaspoon
- Garlic paste – 1 teaspoon
- Salt – to taste

Chettinad masala (Roast and grind)

- Poppy seeds – 1 tablespoon
- Grated coconut – ¼ cup
- Coriander seeds – 1 tablespoon
- Fennel seeds – 1 teaspoon
- Cumin – ¾ teaspoon
- Peppercorns – ½ teaspoon

- Red chilies – 4 to 5
- Cardamoms, green – 3
- Cloves – 4
- Cinnamon stick – 1 inch

Cooking directions:

- Marinate the chicken with turmeric, chili powder, curd, salt, ginger, and garlic paste in a mixing bowl and set aside for 15 minutes.
- In the Instant Pot, select SAUTÉ mode low heat and press start.
- Dry roast coriander seeds and red chilies for a minute. When it starts to release the fragrance, add cardamoms, cumin, pepper, cinnamon, cloves and continue stirring for 2-3 minutes. Finally, add the poppy seeds and roast for 2 minutes. Transfer the contents into a plate.
- In the sauté mode fry the coconut for 2-3 minutes until it releases the aroma.
- Add the contents in a blending jar and make a fine powder, or you can add little water and make a paste.
- Now the masala is ready.
- To prepare the Chettinad dish, in your Instant Pot, select SAUTÉ mode low heat and heat oil for a minute.
- Add bay leaf and chopped onions and continue sautéing for about 3-4 minutes, until it becomes brown and transparent.
- Add the marinated chicken and fry for 5 minutes.
- Now add tomatoes, turmeric, salt, and chili powder.
- Add the masala and curry leaves.
- Pour 1 cup of water.
- Cancel sauté mode by pressing START/STOP.
- Close the lid and pressure valve.
- Select cooking to poultry mode high pressure for 5 minutes.
- When the whistle starts blowing, quick release the pressure.
- Now change the cooking mode to sauté low heat for 10-15 minutes.
- As the sauce thickens, we can add water for the desired consistency. Add curry leaves for a pleasant aroma.
- Serve hot with ghee rice or naan.

Nutritional information:

Calories: 570 | Cholesterol: 125 mg | Sodium: 136 mg | Proteins: 34 grams | Carbs: 13 grams | Potassium: 657mg | Fat: 42g | Dietary fiber: 5g | Sugars: 4g

MUGHLAI ZAAFRANI CHICKEN

Preparation: 10 minutes |Cooking: 40 minutes |Servings: 4

Ingredients:

- Chicken fresh, cut into pieces with bone – 2 pounds

- Soaked Saffron in milk – 12 strands
- Black pepper – 5
- Cinnamon – 1 inch
- Ginger paste – 1 teaspoon
- Garlic paste – 1 teaspoon
- Onion, sliced – 1 cup
- Soaked Cashew nuts – 15
- Kashmiri red chili powder – 2 teaspoons
- Coriander ground – 2 teaspoons
- Garam masala powder – ½ teaspoon
- Ghee – 3 tablespoons
- Oil – 2 tablespoons
- Cloves – 4
- Black /green cardamom – 2
- Salt – to taste
- Kewra essence – 5 drops
- Water – 1 cup

Cooking directions:

- Place an insert pan in the Instant Pot and select SAUTÉ mode.
- In the pan pour some oil and heat up on low temperature.
- When the pan becomes hot add onion and sauté about 4-5 minutes or until it becomes golden brown.
- Keep it aside.
- Again select SAUTÉ mode and pour oil and ghee heat at high temperature.
- When the pan becomes hot add cardamoms, black pepper, cinnamon, and cloves.
- Sauté it for 1-2 minute.
- Increase the temperature and add chicken and fry for 5 minutes.
- In a blender, add fried onions and soaked cashew nuts to make a fine floury paste.
- Add the paste into the cooking chicken and continue cooking for about 5 minutes. Stir occasionally.
- Add ginger, garlic paste with a little salt.
- Fry about 2-3 minutes till the raw smell goes.
- Now, add curd, Kashmiri red chili powder, coriander powder, garam masala powder, and salt.
- Add a cup of water.
- Cancel sauté mode.
- Cover the lid, close the pressure vent and select poultry mode and set the timer for 5 minutes.
- When the timer blows, quick release the pressure from the Instant Pot.
- Open the lid, and add cardamom powder, saffron, and essence and simmer for another 10 minutes.
- Garnish the dish with your choice and serve hot with chapatti or paratha.

Nutritional Values:

Calories: 468 | Carbs: 5g | Cholesterol: 118mg | Potassium: 364mg | Fat: 38g | Protein: 24g | Sodium: 118mg | Dietary fiber: 1g

CHICKEN CURRY WITH COCONUT MILK

Preparation: 40 minutes | Cooking: 30 minutes | Servings: 4

Ingredients:

Marinade section:

- Boneless chicken – 1½ pounds
- Turmeric powder – 2 teaspoons
- White vinegar - 1 teaspoon
- Black pepper powder – ½ teaspoon
- Salt – taste

For paste mix:

- Pearl onions – 10
- Garlic – 5 cloves
- Ginger – one piece
- Fennel seeds – ½ teaspoon

Other items:

- Curry leaves – 10 to 15
- Green chilies, julienned – 4
- Cubed potatoes – 2
- Chopped red onions – 2
- Tomatoes, chopped – 2 medium
- Garam masala powder – 1 teaspoon
- Cumin powder – ½ teaspoon
- Turmeric powder - ½ teaspoon
- Coriander powder – 1 tablespoon
- Red chili powder – ½ teaspoon
- Coconut oil – 2 tablespoons
- Plain coconut milk – 2 cups
- Salt - to taste

For tempering:

- Pearl onion, sliced – 2
- Coconut oil – 2 tablespoons
- Curry leaves – 6-8

Cooking directions:

- Take a medium bowl and marinate the chicken pieces by adding turmeric powder, pepper powder, vinegar and salt, and mix and keep it aside for half an hour.
- Next, crush the pearl onions, garlic, ginger, and fennel seeds and make a paste.
- Now, in the Instant Pot select SAUTÉ mode, add coconut oil and heat on medium-high temperature.
- Add chopped onions, curry leaves, and green chilies and sauté about 3-5 minutes till the onions become transparent and turn golden brown.
- In this stage, add turmeric, coriander, cumin, red chili, and garam masala powders.
- Sauté the mixture well for about 2-3 minutes, until it emanates the fragrance.
- Add the crushed coarse paste and garlic and sauté for about 3-4 minutes till the raw smell disappears.
- Now, add finely chopped tomatoes and add a little salt to make the tomatoes soft.
- Stir and continue sautéing for about 4-5 minutes to make it a paste/pulp form.
- Now, add the marinated chicken pieces and the potatoes with adequate water and salt.
- Stop sautéing.
- Close the lid and pressure valve and select poultry mode.
- Select the time to 5 minutes.
- When the timer whistle beeps, you can quick release the pressure of the Instant Pot.
- Change the cooking mode to sauté and set low heat.
- Now add coconut milk and stir well. Cook for five minutes and stop cooking.
- In another pan, you can prepare the tempering ingredients.
- Sauté coconut oil in a non-stick pan.
- When the pan becomes hot, add chopped pearl onions and curry leaves to it.
- Once the onion turns its color, pour the mixture to the chicken curry. After that, cover the curry with a lid to get the flavor. The tempering will take about 2-3 minutes.
- Serve hot with naan, chapatti, rice or bread.

Nutritional values:

Calories: 735| Fat: 54g | Cholesterol: 166mg | Carbs: 32g| Sugars: 10g| Fiber: 7g | Protein: 32g |Potassium: 1057mg | Sodium: 848mg

CHICKEN TIKKA MASALA

Cooking: 20 minutes | Servings: 2

Ingredients for marinating
- Boneless, skinless chicken – ½ lb. chopped into smaller pieces
- Greek yogurt – ½ cup
- Garam masala – 1 ½ tsps.
- Lemon juice – 1 ½ tsps.
- Black pepper – ½ tsp.
- Ground ginger – ¼ tsp.

For the sauce:

- Canned tomato puree – 7 ounces
- Garlic – 2 cloves, minced
- Garam masala – 2 tsps.
- Paprika – ¼ tsp.
- Turmeric – ¼ tsp.
- Salt – ¼ tsp.
- Cayenne to taste
- Heavy whipping cream – ½ cup

For serving :

- Basmati rice
- Naan
- Freshly chopped cilantro

Cooking directions:

- Except for the chicken, combine all the marinade ingredients in a bowl and mix well.
- Add chicken chunks and coat well. Marinate in the refrigerator for at least 1 hour.
- Press the sauté mode on your Instant Pot (IP).
- Add the chicken and marinade. Sauté until 5 minutes or cooked on all side. Stirring occasionally. Turn off the sauté mode.
- Except for the cream, add all the sauce ingredients to the IP, pour over the chicken.
- Cover and cook at high pressure for 10 minutes at manual.
- Release pressure when cooked.
- Add the cream and mix. Simmer on sauté for a few minutes.
- Serve with basmati rice or naan.

Nutritional values:

Calories: 460, Fat: 27g, Carb: 19g, Protein: 32g

CHICKEN BIRYANI

Cooking: 40 minutes | Servings: 2

Ingredients:

- Garam masala – ½ tsp.
- Ginger – ¼ tbsp. grated
- Garlic – ¼ tbsp. minced
- Red chili powder – ¼ tbsp.
- Turmeric – a pinch
- Mint leaves – a few
- Chopped cilantro - a few
- Lemon juice – ½ tbsp.
- Plain yogurt – 1 tbsp.

- Kosher salt – ½ tsp.
- Chicken – ½ pound, bone-in, skinless (cut into bite-sized pieces)

Remaining ingredients:
- Basmati rice – ¾ cup, extra-long variety (washed and soaked in water)
- Ghee – ¾ tbsp. divided
- Yellow onion – ½, sliced
- Bay leaves- 1
- Salt – ½ tsp.
- Saffron – ¼ tsp. mixed in 1 tbsp. warm milk
- Eggs - 1 ½ boiled and shelled
- Jalapeno – ¼, sliced

Raita:
- Plain yogurt – ½ cup
- Yellow onion – ¼, finely diced
- Tomato – ½ diced
- Kosher salt to taste
- Chopped cilantro – ¼ tsp.

Cooking directions:
- In a bowl, add the mint leaves, turmeric, chili powder, garlic, ginger, garam masala, half of the lemon juice, chopped cilantro, salt, and yogurt.
- Add chicken and coat well. Marinate in the refrigerator for at least 30 minutes.
- Press sauté and add ghee and onions to the hot pot.
- Cook for 10 minutes or until the onion is caramelized.
- Remove and set aside about half of the onion for garnishing.
- Add the rest of the ghee to the Instant Pot and add sliced jalapeno.
- Add half of the marinated chicken, marinated liquid and bay leaf to the pot. Press Cancel and mix well. Deglaze the pot with a spatula and remove all the brown bits from bottom of the pot by scraping.
- Add the remaining chicken and close the lid.
- Press Manual and cook for 4 minutes on High.
- Do a quick release, and open.
- Mix the chicken well and remove any stuck food from the bottom.
- Drain the rice and add to the chicken. Add 1 cup of water and salt. Adjust water if necessary.
- Close and cook on Manual on High for 6 minutes.
- Do a quick release when cooked.
- Open and gently mix the rice and chicken.
- Garnish with saffron liquid and caramelized onions
- Serve with lemon wedges, hard-boiled egg, and Raita.

- To make the Raita: in a bowl, whisk the yogurt. Add salt, tomatoes, and onion and mix well. Garnish with cilantro.

Nutritional values:

Calories: 503, Fat: 18g, Carb: 60g, Protein: 20g

ASIAN CHICKEN AND RICE

Cooking: 10 minutes | Servings: 2

Ingredients:
- Uncooked jasmine rice – ½ cup (drained and rinsed)
- Skinless chicken thighs – 2, boneless
- Salt – ¼ tsp.
- Ground black pepper – 1 pinch
- Peanut oil – ½ tbsp.
- Yellow onion – ¼, chopped
- Minced garlic – 1 ½ cloves
- Minced ginger – 1 tsp.
- Cumin powder – 1 tsp.
- Chicken broth – ½ cup
- Carrot – 1, chopped
- Bell pepper – ½ chopped
- Soy sauce – ½ tbsp.
- Sesame oil – ½ tsp.
- Chopped green onion – 1 tbsp. for garnish

Cooking directions:
- Season the chicken with salt and pepper. Marinate for 10 to 15 minutes.
- Add peanut oil in the Instant Pot.
- Press Sauté and place onion in the pot.
- Stir fry for 3 minutes.
- Add the cumin, ginger, and garlic. Cook until fragrant.
- Turn off sauté and add broth.
- Deglaze the pot if necessary.
- Add the pepper and carrot.
- Spread the rice in the pot evenly.
- Top with chicken. And drizzle with soy sauce. Don't stir.
- Close and press Manual.
- Cook on High for 10 minutes.
- Release pressure naturally.
- Shred the chicken with forks.
- Drizzle with sesame oil.

- Add the sesame seed and green onions.
- Mix and serve.

Nutritional values:

Calories: 417, Fat: 10.9g, Carb: 46g, Protein: 32g

INDIAN BUTTER CHICKEN

Cooking: 25 minutes | Servings: 2

Ingredients:
- Ghee – 1 tbsp.
- Onion – ½ diced
- Minced garlic – 2 tsps.
- Minced ginger – ½ tsp.
- Skinless and boneless chicken thighs – ¾ pound, cut into quarters

Spices:
- Coriander powder – ½ tsp.
- Garam masala – ½ tsp.
- Paprika – ½ tsp.
- Salt – ½ tsp.
- Turmeric – ½ tsp.
- Black pepper – 1 pinch
- Cayenne – 1 pinch
- Ground cumin – 1 pinch
- Tomato sauce – 6 ounces

Add later:
- Chopped green bell peppers
- Heavy cream
- Fenugreek leaves
- Cilantro

Cooking directions:
- Press the sauté and add the ghee and onion to the Instant Pot.
- Stir-fry onions until beginning to brown, about 6 to 7 minutes.
- Add ginger, garlic, and chicken. Stir-fry the chicken until the outside is no longer pink, about 6 to 7 minutes.
- Add the spices and mix.
- Stir in the tomato sauce and cover with the lid.
- Cook on high pressure for 10 minutes.
- Do a quick release and open the lid.
- Press sauté and the bell peppers and cook until soft.
- Stir in the fenugreek leaves and cream.

- Garnish with cilantro and serve.

Nutritional values:

Calories: 243, Fat: 15.7g, Carb: 14.4g, Protein: 12.1g

Meat – Indian Style

Instant Pot Beef Fry Kerala Style

Preparation: 15 mins | Cooking: 1 hour & 20 mins |
Servings: 6

Ingredients

- Beef (cut into small cubes) -2.2 pounds
- Onion, nicely sliced -2 large
- Tomatoes, chopped -2 large
- Ginger paste-2 tablespoons
- Garlic paste-2 tablespoons
- Green chilies-2-3
- Coriander seeds-3 tablespoons
- Fennel seeds-4 tablespoons
- Cloves-8
- Green cardamom seeds-6
- Cinnamon-1" stick
- Black peppercorns-25

For tempering:

- Large onion- 1 (chopped finely)
- Curry leaves-50
- Coconut, (1" julienned) -1 cup
- Mustard seeds-1 tablespoon
- Sunflower/vegetable cooking oil-4 tablespoons

Cooking directions:

- Place the insert pan in your Instant Pot and set the cooking to manual SAUTÉ mode on low heat.
- When the pan becomes hot, put the fennel, cloves, coriander seeds, cardamom seeds, peppercorns, and cinnamon and start roasting for about 5 minutes.
- Stir all the spices occasionally until it gets a slightly darker color and starts to emanate the fragrance.
- Now stop sautéing and let it cool.
- After cooling the ingredients, grind it to a fine powder.
- Into a large bowl, transfer the powdered spices, and add tomatoes, ginger, green chilies, garlic paste, and sliced onions. Combine the spices.
- Now, put the meat and combine with the ingredients and keep it aside.
- Let it marinate for one hour or more.

- Now again in your Instant Pot, select the manual sauté mode.
- When the Insert Pot become hot pour in some cooking oil.
- Now add mustard seeds, curry leaves and wait until it finishes spluttering.
- After that, add the finely chopped onions to it and fry till it becomes translucent.
- Add the sliced coconut into the pan and cook so that it starts to turn a pale yellow color. All these processes will take about 10 minutes.
- Put the marinated meat and the remaining marinade into the insert port and combine with tempering mix.
- Do not add water while cooking as the meat will release enough juice/water.
- Now change the sauté mode to high heat and cook for about 1 hour. Stir occasionally, until the meat becomes brown.
- Remember, the entire dish should turn to a dark brown color.
- It is a dry dish; hence there won't be any gravy in it. So if water is there, make sure to dry it off.
- Serve hot for dinner or lunch.

Nutritional value:

Calories: 496 | Carbohydrate: 20g | Protein: 53g | Fat: 23g |Cholesterol: 149mg | Sodium: 243mg |Dietary fiber: 6g | Calcium: 106mg

GOAN PORK INSTANT POT VINDALOO

Preparation: 30 m minutes | Cooking: 30 minutes|
Servings: 4

Ingredients:

- Boneless pork loin roast,(cut into 1-inch cubes) -2 pounds
- Onions, chopped-4
- Vegetable oil-1/4 cup
- Dried Kashmiri chili peppers, stemmed and seeded-16
- Cinnamon stick-1 (1 inch) piece
- Cumin seeds-1 teaspoon
- Whole cloves-6
- Ground turmeric- ½ teaspoon
- White vinegar-1 tablespoon
- Whole black peppercorns- ½ teaspoon
- Fresh ginger minced- 1 (2 inches)
- Garlic minced-10 cloves
- Boiling water-2 cups
- Green chili peppers, seeded and cut into strips-2
- White vinegar- ¼ cup
- salt to taste

Cooking directions:

- Grind all the ingredients like Kashmiri chilies, cumin, cinnamon stick, clove, turmeric, and peppercorns, with an electric grinder to make it a fine powder.
- Transfer the fine spice powder into a medium bowl.
- Add salt to taste.
- Add white vinegar and combine thoroughly to make a marinade paste.
- Put the chopped pork into the marinade mix and coat the pork evenly.
- Keep the marinated pork in a closed container and refrigerate about 10-12 hours.
- For a better result always marinate for a more extended period.
- In your Instant Pot pan pour vegetable oil.
- Set the cooking to manual high SAUTÉ mode.
- When the oil becomes hot, stir onions for about 3-5 minutes until it turns translucent.
- Now add garlic, ginger and sauté about 10 minutes or until the ingredients become golden brown and the flavour starts to release.
- Now transfer the marinated pork along with the remaining marinade into the Instant Pot.
- Stir continuously and cook for about 5 minutes.
- When the pork starts to become firm, pour in some water.
- Cover the pot, stop sautéing and close vents.
- Select normal meat/stew mode and set the cooking to 15 minutes.
- After 15 minutes, allow the pressure release naturally. It will take about 20-30 minutes.
- By now the pork becomes soft.
- Open the lid and pour in ¼ cup of vinegar and add julienned chili pepper.
- Stir the dish.
- Again set the cooking to sauté mode low heat for 5 minutes.
- When the chili becomes soft, you can add salt to taste.
- Press START/STOP to stop the cooking.
- Your vindaloo is ready. If the sauce is not thick, sauté it some more time until the sauce gets the required consistency.

Nutritional value:

Calories: 264 | Carbohydrate: 9.2g | Protein: 19.7g | Sugars: 6.9g | Fat: 16.4g | Cholesterol: 54mg |Sodium: 51mg | Potassium: 454mg |Dietary fiber: 1.9g

INSTANT POT GOSHT

Preparation: 3¼ hours | Cooking: 40 minutes | Servings: 6-8

Ingredients:

- Mutton (large cut pieces) - 2¼ pounds
- Garlic paste – 2 tablespoons
- Yogurt-1 cup
- Lemon juice-2 tablespoons
- Sunflower oil (or any cooking oil) – 3 tablespoons
- Garam masala- 2 teaspoons

- Cumin powder-1 teaspoon
- Coriander powder-2 teaspoons
- Turmeric powder - ¼ teaspoon
- Green chilies lengthwise cut-4
- Chopped tomatoes-2 medium
- Salt to taste
- Ginger juliennes for garnishing
- Clean chopped fresh coriander to decorate

Cooking directions:

- In a large bowl, combine garlic paste, lemon juice, yogurt, garam masala to a paste.
- Add salt to taste.
- Now marinate the mutton pieces.
- Cover the bowl and marinate for 3 hours. For a better result, you can marinate it for more hours.
- Now pour sunflower oil into the insert pan of your Instant Pot.
- Set cooking mode to manual SAUTÉ medium heat for 3-4 minutes.
- Put green chilies to the pan when the oil becomes hot.
- Continue cooking until the chilies stop spluttering.
- Now put the whole mutton and marinade into the insert pan and cook about 7 minutes by stirring continuously.
- After that, you can add the remaining ingredients such as cumin powder, coriander powder, turmeric powder, and the tomatoes.
- Stir well and continue cooking for 5 minutes.
- Pour some water over the meat.
- Press stop to cancel sauté mode.
- Cover the lid and seal the vent.
- Select MEAT/STEW high-pressure cook option for 20 minutes.
- Once the cooking time has elapsed, allow it to settle for about 20 minutes.
- Maintain the consistency that you like by sautéing or adding water.
- Once the cooking is over, garnish with coriander and ginger julienne.
- Serve hot.

Nutritional value:

Calories: 408 | Carbohydrate: 10g | Protein: 34g | Fat: 25g | Sodium: 244mg | Calcium: 87mg

INSTANT POT/PRESSURE COOKER MUTTON KORMA

Preparation: 10 minutes | Cooking: 40 minutes | Servings: 4

Ingredients:

- Mutton or lamb - 2¼ pounds
- Yogurt-1 cup

- Turmeric - ¼ teaspoon
- Coriander powder-1 tablespoon
- Red chili powder-1 teaspoon
- Cloves- 6
- Cardamoms - 6
- Cinnamon - 2 inch
- Black cardamoms-2
- Green chili slit-1
- Pepper corn-(lightly crushed) - ½ teaspoon
- Fresh ginger garlic paste-1 tablespoon
- Salt – to taste

Other Ingredients

- Onions, sliced – 3 medium
- Oil as needed
- Strand mace or Javithri-1
- Nutmeg - ⅛ teaspoon
- Cardamom ground - ¼ teaspoon
- Ghee – 3 tablespoons
- Water – 2 cups

Cooking directions:

For marinade:

- Clean, wash and drain mutton to marinate.
- In a large bowl, put the mutton and spices such as cinnamon, cardamoms, pepper, and cloves.
- Mix the ingredients with the mutton.
- Now put the remaining spices like red chili powder, coriander powder, turmeric, red chili powder, and salt into the bowl.
- Add the green chili and yogurt.
- Mix all the spices very well with the mutton and keep it aside for at least for two hours. For better results, you can marinate it for extended hours.

Cooking procedure:

- Put some ghee over the marinade and combine it thoroughly.
- Set your Instant Pot to SAUTÉ mode low heat.
- After a minute pour in oil.
- When the oil becomes hot, put the nicely chopped onion and add a little salt.
- Stir continuously and sauté for 2-3 minutes. Adding salt will let the onion cook quickly.
- Continue cooking until the onion becomes golden brown.
- Transfer it to an electric mix, coarsely pulse the onion.
- Put the mutton and marinade into the insert pot and sauté it for about 10 minutes.
- Stop sautéing by pressing START/STOP.

- Now close the lid and seal the vent.
- Change the mode to MEAT/STEW manual pressure cook for 20 minutes.
- Don't bother to add water, as mutton and yogurt will generate the required amount of liquid for cooking.
- After 20 minutes allow it to release the pressure naturally.
- Add water if required and sauté for 4-5 minutes to boil the sauce. (You need to do this only if the consistency is too thick)
- Check its tenderness; if it is not cooked well, you can continue cooking for another 10-20 minutes until it becomes soft.
- Now put nutmeg and mace over it.
- Continue cooking in sauté mode for 2-3 minutes.
- Add ¼ cardamom power at this stage and turn off the stove.
- Allow the mutton korma to settle so that the meat can absorb the spices.
- Serve hot along with rice, chapatti or bread.

Nutritional value:

Calories: 596 | Carbohydrate: 15g | Protein: 24g | Sugars: 7g | Fat: 48g |Cholesterol: 128mg |Sodium: 464mg | Potassium: 559mg | Dietary fiber: 3g

SPICY BEEF CURRY SLOW COOKING

Preparation: 15 minutes | Cooking: 4¾ hours | Servings: 4

Ingredients:

Beef and marinade:

- Beef (small cut pieces) - 2¼ pounds
- Coriander ground – 1 teaspoon
- Turmeric ground - ½ teaspoon
- Cumin ground - ½ teaspoon
- Yogurt - ¾ cup
- Salt – to taste

Curry section:

- Coconut/Sunflower oil – 4 tablespoons
- Coriander ground – 2 tablespoons
- Turmeric ground - ¾ teaspoons
- Cumin ground - 1½ teaspoons
- Onion, sliced -1 large
- Tomatoes, chopped - ¾ pound
- Cardamom ground - 3
- Garam masala-2 teaspoon
- Black pepper, fresh ground - ½ teaspoon
- Dried chilies (whole) -4

- Green chili, fresh (finely chopped) -1
- Garlic, finely chopped - 3 cloves
- Ginger, minced -1 tablespoon
- Tomato paste-2 tablespoons
- Beef stock- 2¼ cup
- Lemon juice -1 lemon
- Cilantro leaves – for garnishing.

Cooking directions:

- In a large bowl, put all the marinade ingredients, except meat and yogurt, and combine well.
- Now add yogurt and mix well forming to a paste.
- Add beef and combine well.
- Cover the bowl and refrigerate it for about two hours. You can marinade it for an extended amount of time, for a better effect.
- Now place an insert pan in the Instant Pot and set the cooking to sauté mode high heat.
- When the pan becomes hot, pour some cooking oil.
- You may add a little cooking oil over the marinated beef and start cooking for about 6 minutes.
- Now add a sliced onion into the cooking pot. Slow down the temperature to low-medium and continue cooking for about 5 minutes.
- Add in the spices like cumin, coriander, cardamom, Garam masala, turmeric, whole and chopped chilies, black pepper, garlic, and ginger. Combine the spices with a spatula.
- Again cook it for 3-4 minutes, until it starts to release the aroma.
- Add some tomato paste, lemon juice, and the stock and bring to a simmer.
- Now close the lid and the vent.
- Now set the cooking to slow mode.
- Set the timer for 5-6 hours. (You can also cook the same on high temperature by setting the pot to 3-4 hours)
- Add little salt and pepper to taste.
- Garnish with cilantro leaves while serving.
- Serve hot along with rice.

Nutritional value:

Calories: 224 | Carbohydrate: 18.5g | Protein: 29.7g | Sugars: 6.9g | Fat: 3.7g |Cholesterol: 1mg |Dietary Fiber: 2.2g | Sugars: 6.9g |Potassium: 234mg |Sodium: 427mg

LAMB CURRY

Cooking: 20 minutes | Servings: 2

Ingredients:

- Cubed lamb stew meat – ½ lb.
- Garlic - 2 cloves, minced
- Fresh ginger – ½ inch, grated

- Coconut milk – 2 tbsps.
- Juice of – ½ lime
- Salt to taste
- Black pepper to taste
- Ghee – ½ tbsp.
- Diced tomatoes – 5 oz.
- Garam masala – 1 ½ tsps.
- Turmeric – 1 pinch
- Onion – 1/3, chopped
- Carrot – 1, chopped
- Zucchini – ½, chopped
- Cilantro to taste, chopped

Cooking directions:

- In a bowl, meat, combine lime juice, sea salt, black pepper, milk, ginger, and garlic. Cover and marinate in the refrigerator for 30 minutes or overnight.
- Add the meat, marinate, ghee, garam masala, tomatoes with their juice, onion, and carrots in the IP.
- Cover and cook on High for 20 minutes.
- Do a natural release.
- Open and press sauté.
- Stir in diced zucchini and simmer for 5 to 6 minutes.
- Garnish with chopped cilantro and serve.

Nutritional value:

Calories: 230, Fat: 9g, Carb: 11g, Protein: 25g

Indian Fish Curry Recipes

Indian Fish Curry

Preparation: 10 minutes | Cooking: 20 minutes | Servings: 3

Ingredients:

- Pieces of firm white fish – 1 pound
- Powdered turmeric – 1 teaspoon
- Yogurt – 2 cups
- Olive oil – 6 teaspoons
- Cumin Seeds – 1 teaspoon
- Asafetida – ½ teaspoon
- Cloves – 2
- Grated ginger – 2 teaspoons
- Coriander powder – 2 teaspoons
- Water – 8 ounces
- Spice mixture – 1 teaspoon
- Pieces of green chilies -4
- Chopped cilantro leaves – 4 teaspoons
- Water – 8 ounces
- Salt – as required

Cooking directions:

- In a medium bowl, put fish fillets, salt, and turmeric.
- Rub salt and turmeric on the fish and keep it aside.
- Add little salt and yogurt in the bowl.
- Set the Instant Pot to sauté mode.
- Pour 2 teaspoons of olive oil and fry the fish fillets for about 4-5 minutes until its color gets changed, then keep it aside.
- Pour rest of the olive oil into the insert pot and when the oil becomes hot, add cumin seeds, asafetida, cloves, and grated ginger. Stir it well for 30 seconds.
- Add yogurt, cook the sauce and add coriander powder for 5 minutes.
- Add 8 ounces of water and sprinkle the salt, spices, mixtures, and chilies.
- Now, add in the fish and close the Instant Pot.
- Seal the vent and select manual low pressure for 5 minutes.
- After hearing the beep sound, stop cooking and allow natural pressure release.
- Open the lid and garnish with cilantro leaves.
- Serve hot.

Nutritional value:

Calories: 278 | Carbohydrate: 9g | Protein: 25g | Fat: 16g |Cholesterol: 91mg | Dietary Fiber: 2g |Sodium: 667mg

INSTANT POT FISH TIKKA

Preparation: 5 minutes | Cooking: 10 minutes | Servings: 4

Ingredients:

- Boneless fish – 8 pieces
- Cumin powder - ½ teaspoon
- Cooking oil – 3 tablespoons
- Lemon juice – 2 tablespoons

Marinade preparation:

- Yogurt thick – 1 cup
- Onion, grind to paste – 1 medium
- Olive oil – 4 tablespoons
- Ginger paste, fresh – 1 tablespoon
- Lemon juice, fresh – 4 tablespoons
- Garlic paste, fresh – 1 tablespoon
- Red food coloring – as required

Required spices:

- Turmeric powder - ½ teaspoon
- Cumin powder – 1 teaspoon
- Coriander powder – 1 teaspoon
- Red chili powder – 1 tablespoon
- Cinnamon ground - ¼ teaspoon
- Nutmeg powder - ¼ teaspoon
- Salt – to taste

Cooking directions:

- Clean and wash the fish. Pat dry.
- In a medium bowl put all the marinade items and combine to make a smooth paste.
- Now add the spices to the paste.
- Put the boneless fish into the marinade mix one by one and coat the paste on all sides of the fish.
- Cover the bowl and refrigerate for one hour. For a better marinade result, keep the fish in the refrigerator for more hours.

Direction for making the Fish:

- In your Instant Pot, place a steam rack.
- Pour some water below the rack level.

- Now put the marinated fish in a baking bowl over the rack.
- Close the Instant Pot and pressure valve.
- Set high-pressure cooking for 4 minutes.
- When hearing the timer beep, quick release the pressure.
- Press cancel to stop cooking and open the pot.
- Remove the fish from the steam rack.
- Add the remaining marinade and sauté for 3-4 minutes.
- Once the fish has reached the desired consistency, remove it a serving plate.
- Sprinkle with cumin powder and drizzle some lemon juice.
- Serve hot.

Nutritional values:

Calories: 134 | Carbohydrate: 4g | Protein: 1g | Fat: 13g |Sodium: 707mg | Sugars: 2g | Cholesterol: 1mg

COCONUT MILK FISH CURRY

Preparation: 10 minutes | Cooking: 15-20 minutes | Servings: 4

Ingredients:

- Fresh fish fillet – ¾ pound
- Sliced Onion – 1
- White mushrooms – 2 cups
- Butter – 1 tablespoon
- Minced ginger – 1½ teaspoon
- Curry powder, mild – 2 tablespoons
- Coconut milk, low fat – 9 ounces
- Chopped green beans – 2 cups
- Sliced carrot – ½ cup
- Oyster sauce – 2 tablespoons
- Soy Sauce – 2 teaspoons
- Water - ½ cup
- Salt – to taste
- Fresh curry leaves – for seasoning
- Mustard seeds – for seasoning

Cooking directions:

- Wash and drain the fish properly.
- Cut it into medium-large size pieces.
- Set your Instant Pot to sauté mode high.
- Add butter when you see the 'hot' display.
- When the butter becomes hot, add ginger, onion and stir it well for 4-5 minutes.

- Change the sauté setting to low and add curry powder and stir well for 2-3 minutes. Let the curry powder mix with ingredients in the pan.
- Add ½ cup of water, soy sauce, coconut milk and mix it.
- Now add mushrooms, green beans, carrot and boil the mixture. Sauté it for 10 minutes for a soft texture.
- Add oyster sauce, and fish.
- Close the Instant Pot and seal the vent.
- Set low-pressure cooking for 4 minutes.
- When the timer beeps, quick release the pressure.
- Now in a small cracking pan, put some oil and bring to medium temperature.
- When the oil becomes hot, put ¼ teaspoon mustard seeds and let it crack.
- After the mustard seed has spluttered, put the fresh curry leaves in. Let it sizzle.
- When the sizzling is over, transfer the entire things into the prepared fish curry.
- Serve hot.

Nutritional values:

Calories: 415 | Carbohydrate: 19.8g | Protein: 29.5g | Fat: 26g | Cholesterol: 118mg | Potassium: 999mg | Dietary fiber: 6.5g | Sugars: 8g | Sodium: 314mg

INSTANT POT FISH COCONUT CURRY

Preparation: 10 minutes | Cooking: 10 minutes | Servings: 4

Ingredients:

- Pieces of Tilapia filets – 1 pound
- Olive oil – 1 tablespoon
- Coconut milk – 12 ounces
- Onion medium size – ½
- Red chili powder - ½ teaspoon
- Coriander powder – 1 tablespoon
- Turmeric ground – ½ teaspoon
- Sliced pepper, green – ½
- Ginger garlic paste – 1 tablespoon
- Sliced yellow pepper – ½
- Cumin powder – 1 teaspoon
- Spice mixture – 1 teaspoon
- Cilantro – 3 sprigs
- Mint leaves – 8
- Lime juice – ½ teaspoon
- Mustard seeds – ½ teaspoon
- Curry leaves – 10
- Salt – to taste

Cooking directions:

- Slice onion and the bell pepper nicely.
- Select sauté mode high in the Instant Pot.
- When the display appears 'hot,' pour oil.
- When the oil becomes hot, put the mustard seeds and let it crack.
- Put the curry leaves to sizzle. All this process will take 2-3 minutes.
- Add ginger and garlic paste and cook for 30 seconds by stirring vigorously.
- Now pour coconut milk and mix carefully. Put the pieces of tilapia, cilantro and mix gently. If you stir vigorously, it can spoil the fish.
- And add mint leaves.
- Press Start/Stop to cease the sauté mode.
- Now close the lid of the instant pot and lock the pressure vent too.
- Set the pressure high on manual mode and cook for 3 minutes.
- Once 3 minutes elapsed, quick release the pressure.
- Open the lid and drizzle lemon juice.
- Serve hot along with rice or bread.

Nutritional values:

Calories: 333 | Cholesterol: 56mg | Carbohydrate: 6g | Protein: 25g | Fat: 24g | Sodium: 660mg | Fat: 17g | Potassium: 627mg | Fiber: 1g | Sugars: 1g

FISH MOLEE

Preparation: 10 minutes | Cooking: 30 minutes | Servings: 4

Ingredients:

- Fish (seer fish/king fish) – 1 pound
- Vegetable oil – 2 tablespoons
- Coconut milk – ½ cup
- Green chilies, sliced to half – 3-4
- Sliced onion – 2 cups
- Kashmiri red chili powder – 2 teaspoons
- Chopped ginger – 1
- Chopped garlic – 5-6 cloves
- Chopped tomato – 1 cup
- Turmeric powder – ½ teaspoon
- Black pepper ground – ½ teaspoon
- Lemon juice – 2 teaspoons
- Curry leaves – 10
- Coriander leaves, fresh
- Water - ½ cup
- Salt – to taste

Cooking directions:
- Select sauté mode in the Instant Pot.
- Wait for a minute and put curry leaves, green chilies, and onion and sauté it for 2 minutes.
- Fry the ingredients until their color changes.
- Add tomato and cook it for less than a minute.
- Now add Kashmiri chili powder, turmeric powder, ground black pepper and continue stirring. Make sure not to burn the spices. Sauté on a low temperature. The total process will take 6-8 minutes.
- When the frying fragrance emanates, pour ½ cup of water and coconut milk into the mix.
- To stop sautéing, press START/STOP icon.
- Add the fish.
- Close the lid and pressure vent.
- Select slow pressure cook for 5 minutes.
- When the timer starts to beep, quick release the pressure.
- Open the lid and add lemon juice.
- Change to sauté mode without closing the lid and cook for two minutes.
- After the beep 'cancel' sautéing and garnish with coriander leaves.
- Serve hot for dinner or lunch.

Nutritional value:

Calories: 388 | Carbohydrate: 16g | Protein: 28g | Fat: 25g | Dietary fiber: 3g |Cholesterol: 62mg | Potassium: 788mg | Sodium: 215mg | Sugars: 5g

INDIAN COCONUT SHRIMP CURRY

Cooking: 20 minutes | Servings: 2

Ingredients:
- Shrimp, deveined tail-on – ½ lb.
- Oil – ½ tbsp.
- Mustard seeds – ½ tsp.
- Green chili pepper – 1, sliced
- Onion – ½ cup, chopped
- Ginger – 1 tsp. minced
- Garlic – 1 tsp. minced
- Tomato – ½ cup, chopped
- Coconut milk – 4 oz.
- Lime juice – ½ tbsp.
- Cilantro – 1 tsp.

Spices:
- Ground turmeric – ¼ tsp.
- Cayenne – ½ tsp.

- Garam masala – ¼ tsp.
- Coriander powder – ½ tsp.
- Salt – ¼ tsp.

Cooking directions:

- Press the Sauté on your Instant Pot and add oil and mustard seeds.
- Sizzle for a few seconds, then add the garlic, ginger, onions, and green chili.
- Stir-fry until onions are golden brown, about 5 minutes.
- Add the spices and tomato and mix. Stir-fry for 3 minutes.
- Add the shrimp and coconut milk to the pot. Stir and press cancel.
- Close the lid and press Manual.
- Cook on low pressure for 3 minutes.
- Do a natural release and open the lid.
- Stir in lime juice and garnish with cilantro.
- Enjoy with rice.

Nutritional value:

Calories: 226, Fat: 10g, Carb: 8gm, Protein: 24g

PRESSURE COOKED COCONUT FISH CURRY

Cooking: 10 minutes | Servings: 2

Ingredients:
- Fish fillets or steaks – ½ lb. cut into bite size pieces
- Tomato – ½, chopped
- Green chilies – 1, sliced
- Onion – ½, chopped
- Garlic – 1 clove, minced
- Grated ginger – 1 tsp.
- Curry leaves – 2
- Ground coriander – ½ tsp.
- Ground turmeric – 1 pinch
- Chili powder – a pinch
- Ground fenugreek a pinch
- Unsweetened coconut milk – ½ cup
- Salt to taste
- Lemon juice to taste

Cooking directions:

- Preheat the pressure cooker.
- Add oil and drop the curry leaves.
- Fry for 1 minute.

- Add the ginger, garlic, and onion and sauté until onion is soft.
- Add all the ground spiced and sauté for 2 minutes.
- Deglaze the pot with coconut milk.
- Add fish pieces, tomato, and green chili. Mix.
- Cover and cook on 5 minutes on Low.
- Do a natural release.
- Add salt, and lemon juice before serving.
- Serve.

Nutritional value:

Calories: 160, Fat: 4.1g, Carb: 5.3g, Protein: 23.6g

Rice Indian Recipes

Chicken Biriyani

Preparation: 30 minutes | Cooking: 25 minutes | Servings: 4

Ingredients:

- Basmati rice, long grain – 3 cups
- Chicken – 2 ½ pounds
- Yogurt – 2 cups
- Water – 3 cups
- Cooking oil – 1 cup
- Ghee – 2 tablespoons
- Garlic and ginger paste- 1 teaspoon
- Red pepper – 2 teaspoons
- Biryani spices– 4 teaspoons
- Bay leaves – 2
- Chopped red onions -2
- Salt –to taste

Cooking directions:

- Prepare the marinade in a bowl by mixing garlic and ginger paste, red pepper, biriyani spices, yogurt and salt.
- Add chicken and marinate evenly.
- Refrigerate the marinade for 30 minutes.
- In your Instant Pot, select sauté mode high temperature.
- When the display appears 'hot,' add cooking oil and chopped onion.
- Sauté for 10 minutes until it becomes golden brown.
- Keep a ¼ portion of the golden brown onion in a separate bowl for garnishing biriyani.
- Pour 2 tablespoons of ghee to the remaining onion in the pot.
- Add bay leaves and half portion of the marinated chicken along with the marinade sauce.
- Combine the chicken with the onion thoroughly and also deglaze the pan with the spatula. Remove all the possible brown onions stuck to the side of the Instant Pot.
- When all the brown portions have been cleaned from the pot, add the remaining chicken along with marinade sauce.
- Press START/STOP to cease sautéing.
- Close the Instant Pot and pressure valve.
- Select manual pressure cook for 5 minutes.
- Use quick release when you hear the beep sound.
- Open the lid and gently put in the washed rice.
- Pour 3 cups of water in.

- Add salt and stir.
- Close the lid and select manual pressure cook for 6 minutes.
- When hearing the timer beep, opt for the quick pressure release.
- If the top layer of the rice is not cooked well, you may gently mix the rice to the bottom of the chicken.
- Close the lid for some time so that rice will get cooked thoroughly.
- Before serving, garnish with caramelized onion.
- Serve biryani hot.

Nutritional value:

Calories: 2080 | Carbohydrate: 232g | Protein: 137g | Sugars: 34g | Fat: 68g | Cholesterol: 399mg | Sodium: 760mg |Dietary fiber: 22g

JEERA RICE

Preparation: 5 minutes | Cooking: 10 minutes | Servings: 2

Ingredients:

- Vegetable oil- 2 tablespoons
- Cooking oil – 1 cup
- Cumin(whole) – ½ teaspoon
- White basmati rice -2 cups
- Water – 2½ cups
- Salt –to taste

Cooking directions:

- Wash the rice, drain and keep aside.
- Select sauté mode high in the Instant Pot.
- When the display appears 'hot,' pour oil and put cumin seeds in.
- Sauté it until it starts to splutter for 2-3 minutes. Do not let it burn or turn dark brown.
- Add rice in the sauté pan and fry it about 1 minute
- After that add salt and water.
- Pres START/STOP to stop sauté mode.
- Close the Instant Pot and seal the vent.
- Select manual low pressure for 5 minutes.
- When the timer beeps, quick release the pressure.
- Open the lid and fluff the rice and allow it to settle.
- Serve hot for good taste.

Nutritional value:

Calories: 927 | Carbohydrate: 148g | Protein: 13g | Sugars: 0.3g | Fat: 29g | Cholesterol: 0 mg |Fiber: 3g |Sodium: 166mg

Ghee Rice

Preparation: 5 minutes | Cooking: 15 minutes | Servings: 3

Ingredients:

- Basmati rice – 1½ cup
- Ghee– 3 tablespoons
- Onion, sliced – ½ cup for garnishing
- Sliced onion- ½ cup for rice
- Water – 2 cups
- Ginger paste - ¼ teaspoon
- Cashew – ½ cup
- Raisins - ¼ cup
- Biryani flower -1
- Sauf (fennel seeds) - ½ teaspoon
- Bay leaf -1
- Cloves - 4
- Cinnamon sticks -2 inches long
- Salt to taste

Cooking directions:

- Wash rice and drain water and soak it for 30 minutes.
- In your Instant Pot, select sauté mode high.
- Pour in ghee and when ghee becomes hot add cashews and stir continuously for 3-4 minutes to fry until they becomes golden color. Keep it aside.
- After that add raisins, and stir, until it swells up. Transfer it into a plate and keep it aside.
- Do the same process with onions and after frying them to a golden brown keep them aside on a plate. Onions, cashew and raisins are for garnishing purpose.
- In the same pan mix all spices and stir them continuously and take care not to let them burn.
- Further, add garlic paste in it stir for a while.
- Add rice to this mixture and fry for 2 to 3 minutes. Stir the mixture gently else rice will break.
- Stop sauté mode by pressing START/STOP.
- Pour in water and salt.
- Close the Instant Pot lid and seal the pressure vent.
- Select manual pressure and cook for 5 minutes.
- When the timer beeps, quick release the pressure.
- Open the lid and fluff the rice gently.
- Allow it to settle.
- Before serving, garnish it with cashew, raisins, and onion.
- For delicious and soft ghee rice, serve hot.

Nutritional value:

Calories: 585 | Carbohydrate: 91 g | Protein: 9 g | Sugars: 2 g | Fat: 20 g | Cholesterol: 38mg |Sodium: 23mg |Potassium: 335mg

LEMON RICE

Preparation: 15 minutes | Cooking: 10 minutes | Servings: 5

Ingredients:

- Cooked brown basmati rice -3 cups
- Kosher salt – ¾ teaspoon
- Canola oil – 2 tablespoons
- Lemon juice – ¼ cup
- Black mustard seeds - ½ teaspoon
- Cashew/peanuts - ⅓ cup
- Sliced garlic -2 cloves
- Green chili, small - 1
- Cumin seeds - ½ teaspoon
- Fresh curry leaves -10 leaves
- Chana dal, roasted (split chickpeas) - 2 tablespoons
- Urad dal (split black gram) – 1 tablespoon
- Ground turmeric – ¼ teaspoon

Cooking directions:

- In a bowl, mix salt and lemon juice. Mix until salt dissolves in the lemon juice.
- In the Instant Pot, select sauté mode high.
- When the display appears 'hot,' pour oil.
- Put mustard seed to splutter.
- After spluttering, select the sauté mode to low and add the remaining mustard seeds, chili, pepper, cumin seeds, garlic, curry leaves, chana dal, and urad dal. Sauté for about 3-4 minutes.
- Add cashew/peanuts into the pot and stir for about 2-3 minutes.
- Now press START/STOP to cease heating and add turmeric, lemon juice, and rice and mix it properly to get delicious lemon rice.
- Serve hot.

Nutritional value:

Calories: 220 | Carbohydrate: 29g | Protein: 4g | Sugars: 2g | Fat: 11g | Cholesterol: 0 mg |Protein: 4g | Fiber: 2g | Calcium: 11mg | Sodium: 170mg | Potassium: 79mg

SOUTH INDIAN CURD RICE

Preparation: 5 minutes | Cooking: 15 minutes | Servings: 2

Ingredients:

- Curd/yogurt- 1½ cup

- White rice - ¼ cup
- Brown rice - ¼ cup
- Salt to taste
- Water - 1½ cup

Vegetables for curd rice:

- Grated carrot -2 tablespoons
- Cucumber, grated – ¼ cup
- Coriander leaves, fresh – finely chopped - ¼ cup

Curd rice tempering:

- Hing (asafetida) – pinch
- Green or red chili, julienned - 1
- Urad dal (split black gram) - 1 teaspoon
- Mustard - ½ teaspoon
- Ginger crushed - ½ teaspoon
- Cumin - ½ teaspoon
- Chana dal (split chickpeas) - ¾ teaspoon
- Curry leaves -1 sprig

Cooking directions:

- Wash rice and soak it for 20 -30 minutes.
- After soaking, drain the rice and keep ready.
- Pour 1½ cup of water in the Instant Pot Cooker.
- Put the rice and add salt as required.
- Cover the Instant Pot lid and also seal the pressure vent.
- Select the high-pressure manual for 5 minutes.
- When the timer beeps, quick release pressure.
- Cool it completely and if you wish you can mash it lightly.
- Add curd to the prepared rice and mix it thoroughly.
- Press START/STOP to stop sautéing.
- Put another insert pan in the Instant Pot.
- Select sauté low and when the display shows 'hot,' pour oil.
- When the oil becomes hot, put cumin and mustard seed. When they start to splutter, add urad dal and Chana dal.
- Fry until it becomes golden brown for about 3-4 minutes.
- Soon after that add ginger, chili and curry leaves and sauté for 1 minute.
- After the curry leaves have sizzled, add one pinch of asafetida and sauté for 1 minute.
- Press START/STOP to cease sautéing.
- Add all the ingredients of vegetable for curd to the seasoning mix and stir and transfer to the yogurt rice.
- The South Indian style curd rice is ready to serve.

Nutritional value:

Calories: 310 | Carbohydrate: 49 g | Protein: 11 g | Sugars: 11 g | Fat: 7 g | Cholesterol: 26 mg | Sodium: 126mg | Potassium: 445mg | Dietary fiber: 1g

INDIAN LEMON RICE

Cooking: 20 minutes | Servings: 2

Ingredients
- Basmati rice – ½ cup, soaked for 30 minutes and rinsed
- Olive oil – 1 ½ tbsp.
- Black mustard seeds – ½ tsp.
- Split chickpeas – ½ tbsp.
- Split and skinless black lentils – 1/2 tbsp.
- Raw peanuts – 2 tbsp.
- Curry leaves – 5
- Green chili – 1, sliced
- Minced ginger – ½ tsp.
- Salt – ½ tsp.
- Coriander powder – ½ tsp.
- Turmeric – 1 pinch
- Lemon juice – 1 tbsp.
- Lemon zest – 1 tsp.
- Water – 1 cup

Cooking directions:
- Press the sauté button on the IP and add the oil.
- Add the black lentils, chickpeas and mustard seeds in the hot oil. Stir-fry for 2 minutes. Add the raw peanuts and stir-fry for 2 minutes.
- Add the salt, turmeric, coriander, ginger, green chilies, and curry leaves and stir-fry for 30 seconds.
- Add the rice, water, lemon juice, and zest. Mix well.
- Cover with the lid and cook on high pressure for 6 minutes.
- Do a natural release for 10 minutes.
- Fluff the rice with a fork and serve.

Nutritional value:

Calories: 332, Fat: 8g, Carb: 55g, Protein: 7g

BEANS RECIPES

BEANS THORAN

Preparation: 15 minutes | Cooking: 13 minutes | Serves: 8

Ingredients:

- Green beans, cut into small pieces – ½ pound
- Red chili, cut into half - 1
- Green chili, cut into small rounds – 1
- Grated coconut – ½ cup
- Mustard seeds – 1 teaspoon
- Chili powder – 1 teaspoon
- Cumin seeds - ½ teaspoon
- Olive oil – 1 tablespoon
- Salt - taste

Cooking directions:

- Select SAUTÉ mode high temperature in the Instant Pot.
- When the display shows 'hot,' pour a tablespoon of olive oil.
- Once the oil becomes hot add mustard seed to pop.
- Then add red chili and stir continuously for 2-3 minutes.
- When the aroma of chili emanates, stir in green beans.
- Now add salt, chili powder, grated coconut along with cumin seeds.
- Cover and cook for 8-10 minutes in low heat.
- Once the green beans are tender, turn off the heat and serve the dish hot with rice or roti as preferred.

Nutritional value:

Calories: 85 | Total Fats: 4.2g | Net Carbs: 11.3g | Protein: 3.1g | Fiber: 0.7g | Cholesterol: 0g | Sodium: 10.9mg | Potassium: 3.1mg | Sugars: 0g

SPICY GREEN BEANS

Preparation: 15 minutes | Cooking: 7 minutes | Serves: 4

Ingredients:

- Green beans, fresh, chopped into 1 inch pieces – 1 pound
- Red chili, dried and crushed – 1
- Vegetable oil - ¼ cup
- Mustard seed – 1 tablespoon
- Sugar - ½ teaspoon

- Garlic, finely chopped – 4 cloves
- Black pepper ground - ½ teaspoon
- Salt – to taste
- Water – 1 cup

Cooking directions:

- In your Instant Pot, select SAUTÉ mode high.
- When the display appears 'hot,' pour oil.
- When the oil becomes hot, add mustard seed to splutter.
- Now add chopped dry chili and stir for 2-3 minutes.
- When the chili changes its color to dark, add the chopped garlic, black pepper and stir for about 1-2 minutes until the garlic becomes brown.
- Stop sautéing by pressing START/STOP
- Pour water.
- Add the chopped green beans, salt, and sugar.
- Close the Instant Pot lid and pressure vent.
- Select PRESSURE COOK low mode for 2 minutes.
- Quick release the pressure when the timer beeps.
- Open the cover and allow to settle the heat.
- Serve hot.

Nutritional values:

Calories: 171 | Cholesterol: 0mg | Sodium: 589mg | Carbohydrates: 10.7g | Dietary Fiber: 4.7g | Protein: 2.9g | Potassium: 255mg | Sugars: 2g

BEANS PATOLI CURRY

Preparation: 120 minutes | Cooking: 25 minutes | Serves: 8

Ingredients:

- Green beans – ½ pound
- Red chili – 1 teaspoon
- Chickpeas – ¼ pound
- Turmeric ground – ½ teaspoon
- Green chilis – 4
- Cooking oil – 2 tablespoons
- Cumin seeds – 1 teaspoon
- Asafetida – ¼ teaspoon
- Mustard – 1 teaspoon
- Curry leaves – 5-6 leaves
- Salt – 1 teaspoon
- Coriander leaves – 4-5 leaves
- Urad dal (black gram) – 3 teaspoon

Cooking directions:

- Start the cooking process by soaking the black gram in a medium bowl for about 2 hours.
- In the Instant Pot select SAUTE.
- Pour oil with the display shows 'hot.'
- Now, add the mustard, and let it splutter.
- After spluttering add urad dal (black gram), 2 chilies (red), cumin seeds and the curry leaves and fry it for 2 minutes until the aroma starts to rise.
- Press START/STOP and cease sautéing.
- Cut the green beans into small sizes (2cms) as needed. Remove both ends.
- Wash and drain the Bengal gram and discard the water.
- Using a grinder, mix the spices like the red chili (8), curry leaves, around 4 green chilies, cumin seeds, asafetida, salt, and turmeric powder without adding water.
- Now, marinate the chopped beans with the spice mix.
- In your Instant Pot, select SAUTÉ high mode.
- When the display appears 'hot,' put the beans with spice mix into the pan and sauté for 4-5 minutes.
- Let the beans cook for around 15 minutes to make it soft and tender.
- Once done, let it cool and mash the mixture vigorously to turn it into a dry paste.
- Cover the pan with a lid and let it cook for another 3 minutes.
- Once cooked, open the lid and garnish with chopped coriander leaves.
- Serve it hot.

Nutritional value:

Calories: 87.81 | Total Fats: 7g | Net Carbs: 5.41 | Protein: 1.81g | Fiber: 1.89g | Cholesterol: 6.79g | Sodium: 4.6mg | Potassium: 1mg | Sugars: 0.65g

CLUSTER **B**EANS **F**RY

Preparation: 10 minutes | Cooking: 20 minutes | Serves: 4

Ingredients:

- Green beans – ¾ pounds
- Cooking oil – 1 tablespoon
- Carom seeds, crushed – ¼ teaspoon
- Turmeric powder - ¼ teaspoon
- Asafetida – ¼ teaspoon
- Coriander ground - 1½ teaspoon
- Cumin powder – ½ teaspoon
- Chili powder (red) – 1 teaspoon
- Sugar – 1 teaspoon
- Ginger garlic paste – 2 teaspoons
- Water – ¼ cup

- Fresh coriander leaves – 2 teaspoons
- Salt – 1 teaspoon

Cooking directions:

- Wash and cut the green beans into half inch size.
- On an Instant Pot, select SAUTÉ mode high.
- Pour oil, when the 'hot' display appears.
- Once the oil becomes hot, add the crushed carom seeds, turmeric powder, asafetida, and the ginger garlic paste.
- Sauté the mixture for 2-3 minutes until it starts to release the aroma.
- After sautéing, add sugar, red chili powder and the cumin-coriander powder in the pot. Let it cook for another minute.
- Add the finely chopped beans in the pan and stir it vigorously to let the mixture cover the beans entirely.
- Add ¼ cup water in the pan as you see the dish drying up and continue to stir the mix.
- Stop sautéing by pressing the START/STOP button.
- Close the lid and seal pressure valve.
- Select pressure cooker manual high for 5 minutes.
- When the timer beeps, release the pressure naturally.
- Open the lid and stir the dish.
- The cluster beans are ready to serve.

Nutritional value:

Calories: 57 | Total Fats: 13g | Net Carbs: 2g | Protein: 0.5g | Fiber: 1.89g | Cholesterol: 8g | Sodium: 5mg | Potassium: 0mg | Sugars: 3.6g

GREEN BEANS WITH POTATOES

Preparation: 10 minutes | Cooking: 15 minutes | Serves: 5

Ingredients:

- Green beans chopped – 3½ cups
- Potatoes – 2 small
- Cooking oil – 2 teaspoons
- Asafetida – ¼ teaspoon
- Mustard seeds – ½ teaspoon
- Garlic – 3 cloves
- Red chili powder – ¼ teaspoon
- Turmeric ground – ½ teaspoon
- Cumin ground – ½ teaspoon
- Coriander ground – ½ tablespoon
- Salt – to taste
- Water – ¼ cup

- Fresh cilantro, chopped – as required for garnishing.
- Lemon juice (fresh) – 2 teaspoons

Cooking directions:

- Wash and cut the beans in generous size by removing both ends.
- Try to keep the pieces limited to ¼ inch long or smaller as needed. The smaller the size, the quicker it will cook. However, the size entirely depends upon you.
- Peel potatoes and dice into ¾ inch pieces.
- Let us cook it in an instant pot.
- Select 'SAUTÉ' (normal) mode on the Instant Pot.
- When the Instant Pot displays 'hot,' pour cooking oil in first and when the oil becomes hot add the following ingredient like mustard seeds, minced garlic, and asafetida. Let the mixture fry for 2 minutes before adding another batch.
- Once done, add the green beans, red chili powder, ground turmeric and diced potato in the mix alongside ¼ teaspoon of salt and stir it well to let the spices absorb into the beans and potatoes. Cook it for 2 minutes.
- After a while, you may add water to the mix and close the lid. Set the timer of 2 minutes using the 'sauté' button on the pot.
- Once the time has elapsed, let the pressure release naturally for about 5 minutes and later on manually release the pressure.
- Again select sauté mode and cook the vegetables for 2 minutes.
- Once you feel the potatoes and the beans are tender enough, add the ground coriander and ground cumin and continue to stir.
- Mix it well and let it stay on low heat for extra 2-3 minutes.
- Add salt to taste and freshly squeezed lemon juice at the top.
- Press START/STOP to cease sautéing.
- Garnish it with freshly cut cilantro.
- Serve hot.

Nutritional value:

Calories: 99 | Total Fats: 2g | Net Carbs: 14g | Protein: 6g | Fiber: 0.5g | Cholesterol: 0g | Sodium: 1g | Potassium: 7mg | Sugars: 0g

DAL RECIPES

Guajarati Dal

Preparation: 10 minutes | Cooking: 20 minutes | Servings: 4

Ingredients:

- Turmeric powder - ½ teaspoon
- Tuvar dal (split red gram) - 1 cup
- Chili powder - ½ teaspoon
- Green chili paste - ½ teaspoon
- Chopped tomato - ½ cup
- Grated jaggery - 1 teaspoon
- Ginger paste - ½ teaspoon
- Boiled peanuts - 2 tablespoons
- Lemon juice - 2 tablespoons
- Chopped coriander - 2 tablespoons
- Salt- as per taste
- Water – 4 cups

For tempering:

- Hing (asafetida) - ¼ teaspoon
- Ghee - 2 tablespoons
- Mustard seeds - ½ teaspoon
- Fenugreek seeds - ¼ teaspoon
- Dry red chilies - 2 to 3
- Cumin seeds - ½ teaspoon
- Cinnamon - 1 inch
- Cloves - 2 to 3

Cooking Directions:

- Select sauté mode in the Instant Pot.
- Add the mentioned amount ghee when the pot signals 'hot.'
- Once the ghee starts to melt, add mustard seed. When it begins spluttering add fenugreek seeds, Hing (asafetida), and cumin seeds and keep stirring them continuously for a minute.
- After a minute, add cloves, dry red chili, and cinnamon stick to the pan and fry it for a minute as well.
- Stop sautéing by pressing the START/STOP button.
- Put washed tuvar dal (split red gram) in the Instant Pot.
- Add red chili powder, turmeric powder, tomato, ginger paste and green chili paste to the pressure cooker.

- Add about four cups of water and add salt to taste.
- Close the lid and also seal the pressure valve.
- Select PRESSURE COOK manual high for 15 minutes.
- When the timer beeps, go for a natural pressure release.
- Once the pressure has released naturally, open the cooker and whisk the dal.
- Add lemon juice, jaggery, and boiled peanuts to the dal.
- Before serving, mix them well.
- Garnish using fresh coriander leaves.
- Serve hot along with steamed rice or phulka (chapatti).

Nutritional Value:

Calories: 262 | Carbohydrate: 34g | Protein: 13g | Sugars: 4g | Fat: 8g | Dietary Fiber: 15g | Cholesterol: 19mg | Sodium: 55mg | Potassium: 587mg

INSTANT POT DAAL TADKA

Preparation: 15 minutes | Cooking: 5 minutes | Servings: 6

Ingredients:

- Moong dal (split green gram) - ½ cup
- Chana dal (split chickpeas) - ½ cup
- Garlic - 2 cloves
- Masoor dal (split red lentil) - ½ cup
- Cumin seeds - 1 tablespoon
- Green chili - 1 large
- Turmeric powder - ¼ teaspoon
- Extra virgin olive oil - 1½ tablespoon
- Tomato - 1 large
- Water - 4 cups
- Salt – to taste

Cooking Directions:

- On the Instant Pot, select SAUTÉ mode high.
- Pour about one and a half tablespoons of olive oil when the display signals 'hot.'
- When the oil becomes hot, add chopped garlic, cumin seeds, and chopped chili to the pan and wait until the cumin seeds pop up. It will take about 1-2 minutes.
- Now stop sautéing by pressing START/STOP button.
- In the Instant Pot mix, add washed moong dal, chana dal and masoor dal as per the mentioned quantity.
- Put the finely diced tomato to the pot and add water.
- Add salt to taste.
- Close the lid and seal the pressure valve.
- Select PRESSURE COOK high manual for 8 minutes.

- When the timer beeps, go for a natural pressure release, which is about 10 minutes.
- Open the top and mash the cooked lentils.
- Before serving, add some finely chopped cilantro above for garnishing.

Nutritional Value:

Calories: 118.9 | Carbohydrate: 15.3g | Protein: 5.5g | Fat: 4.8g | Dietary Fiber: 3.6g | Cholesterol: 0.1mg | Sodium: 479.3mg

DAAL MAKHANI

Preparation: 5 minutes | Cooking: 25 minutes | Servings: 4

Ingredients:

- Tomatoes, crushed tomatoes - 14 ounces
- Dry lentils (red lentils) - 1 cup
- Fresh ginger, grated - 1 tablespoon
- Garlic, minced - 1 tablespoon
- Cayenne pepper - 1 teaspoon
- Unsalted butter - 4 tablespoons
- Water - 3 cups
- Heavy cream - ⅓ cup
- Fresh cilantro, minced - 2 tablespoons
- Fresh black pepper ground - as required
- Salt - as per taste

Cooking Directions:

- In the Instant Pot, select sauté mode high.
- When it becomes 'hot,' add unsalted butter, minced garlic, black pepper ground, cayenne pepper, and fresh ginger. Sauté for about 2 minutes, until you can feel the aroma.
- Add tomatoes and cook about 3 minutes, until it becomes soft pulp.
- Stop sautéing mode by pressing START/STOP.
- Put the mentioned amount of lentils in and pour in 3 cups of water.
- Close the lid and seal the pressure valve.
- Select PRESSURE COOK high manual for 8 minutes.
- When the timer gives a warning beep, go for a natural pressure release.
- Open the lid and mash the cooked lentils.
- Check the consistency of the mixture, and if required, cook on sauté mode low for about 5-10 minutes, depending on the consistency requirements.
- Press START/STOP to cancel sautéing.
- Stir in the cream and then garnish it with cilantro before serving.

Nutritional Value:

Calories: 263 | Carbohydrate: 18.5g | Protein: 6.7g | Fat: 19.1g | Dietary Fiber: 5.7g | Cholesterol: 58mg | Sodium: 262mg

PANJABI **D**AL **T**ADKA

Preparation: 10 minutes | Cooking: 15 minutes | Servings: 4

Ingredients:

- Moong dal (split green gram) - ½ cup
- Arhar dal (split red gram) - ½ cup
- Oil - 2 tablespoons
- Ginger, grated - 1 teaspoon
- Onion, chopped - ½ cup
- Green chili, chopped - 1 teaspoon
- Turmeric powder - ½ teaspoon
- Chopped tomato - ½ cup
- Red chili powder - 1 teaspoon
- Lemon juice - 1 tablespoon
- Water – 3 cups
- Salt - as required
- Cumin seeds - 1 teaspoon
- Ghee - 2 tablespoons
- Hing (asafetida) - ¼ teaspoon
- Chopped garlic - 2 teaspoons
- Red chilies, dry - 2 to 3
- Fresh coriander - 2 tablespoons

Cooking Directions:

- Set your Instant Pot to sauté mode high.
- Add ghee when the display shows 'hot.'
- Put cumin seeds, chopped garlic, ginger, and asafetida and sauté for 2 minutes until the chopped garlic becomes light brown.
- Add dry red chilies sauté for 1 minute until it releases the aroma.
- Now add onion and sauté it for 2-3 minute until it becomes light golden brown.
- Now, add tomato and green chili and cook it for another two to three minutes
- Add red chili powder and turmeric powder to the pan.
- Press START/STOP to cancel sautéing.
- Put washed and drained dal into the Instant Pot.
- Pour three cups of water into the cooker and salt as per your taste requirement.
- Close the lid and seal the pressure vent.
- Select PRESSURE cook manual high for 5 minutes.
- When the timer beeps, go for a natural pressure release.
- The pressure will release naturally within 5 minutes.

- Open the top and mash the dal using the backside of a ladle.
- Sprinkle lemon juice into the pan and mix well.
- Garnish the dal with freshly chopped coriander leaves and serve hot.

Nutritional Value:

Calories: 129 | Carbohydrate: 6g | Protein: 1g | Sugars: 2g | Fat: 11g | Cholesterol: 28mg | Potassium: 168mg | Dietary Fiber: 1g | Sodium: 25mg

INSTANT POT DAL FRY

Preparation: 2 minutes | Cooking: 15 minutes | Servings: 1

Ingredients:

- Green pepper (also known as bell peppers) - ¼ cup
- Chopped onions - ¼ cup
- Ghee - 1 tablespoon
- Diced tomatoes - 1
- Cumin seeds - 1 teaspoon
- Washed toor dal (split red gram) - ½ cup
- Onion, thinly chopped - ½
- Cinnamon - 1 teaspoon
- Garlic – 3 cloves
- Curry leaves – 6
- Green chili pepper, split sliced - 1
- Hing (Asafetida) - ¼ teaspoon
- Water – 3 cups
- Coriander leaves fresh – to garnish

Cooking Directions:

- On the Instant Pot, select sauté mode high.
- Add oil when the display shows 'hot.'
- When the oil becomes hot add cumin seeds, garlic cloves, cinnamon, green chili, asafetida, and curry leaves.
- Sauté for about 2 minutes until the garlic becomes light brown.
- Now add chopped onion and sauté for 2 minutes, until it becomes golden brown.
- Add the chopped tomato and continue sautéing for another 2 minutes.
- Put the washed toor dal in and combine all.
- Pour in water and add salt.
- Press START/STOP to cancel sauté mode.
- Close the lid and seal the pressure vent.
- Select Pressure cook manual high for 5 minutes.
- When the timer beeps, release the pressure naturally. It will take about 5 minutes.
- Open the top, add salt to taste and garnish with fresh coriander leaves.

Nutritional Value:

Calories: 196.1 | Carbohydrate: 31.4g | Protein: 7.4g | Fat: 6.1g | Cholesterol: 0.0mg | Sodium: 15.2mg | Dietary Fiber: 9.5g

VEGETABLE RECIPES

SOUTH INDIAN SAMBAR

Preparation: 10 minutes | Cooking: 15 minutes | Servings: 4 to 5

Ingredients:

For Sambar Recipe:

- Toor dal (split red gram) - 1 cup
- Sambar powder – 2 tablespoons
- Turmeric powder - ½ teaspoon
- Coconut, fresh, grated - ¼ cup
- Red chili powder – 1 teaspoon
- Tamarind paste - 1 to 2 tablespoons
- Salt - as per taste
- Coriander leaves - ¼ cup
- Cooking oil – 2 tablespoons
- Water – 4 cups

Vegetables: (Chop all the vegetables to moderate size)

- Drumsticks - 1 to 2
- Shallots - 12 to 15
- Red pumpkin - 3 to 4
- Ladies' fingers (Okra) - 2 to 3
- Chopped tomato - 1 medium
- Green chili - 1
- Carrots – 2
- Beans – 12-15
- Potatoes - 3

For Tempering:

- Curry leaves - 1 sprig
- Oil or ghee - 2 tablespoon
- Mustard seeds - ½ teaspoon
- Jeera (cumin) - ½ teaspoon
- Hing (asafetida) - 2 pinches
- Methi seeds (Fenugreek seeds) - 1 pinch
- Dry red chili – 1

Cooking Directions:

- Make a fine coconut paste by adding little water in an electric mixer. Keep it ready to use.
- In your Instant Pot, select sauté mode high.
- Pour cooking oil when the display illuminates 'hot.'
- Add tempering ingredients starting with mustard seed, cumin, fenugreek and sauté for 1-2 minutes.
- Now add asafetida, dry red chili and sauté for 1 minute. Let the dry red chili become dark brown to release the aroma.
- Finally, put in curry leaves and sizzle.
- Add the chopped vegetables and cook for about 2-3 minutes until the vegetables become soft. The taste and flavor of the sambar will be delicious if all of the vegetables are soft cooked.
- Now add the washed lentils, turmeric powder, sambar powder, tamarind pulp/extract, coconut paste, water, and salt.
- Combine it. Make sure the salt and tamarind are in the right quantities.
- Press START/STOP button to cancel the sauté mode.
- Close the lid and pressure valve.
- Select PRESSURE cook manual high for 8 minutes.
- When the timer blows, go for a natural pressure release.
- Open the top and garnish with fresh chopped coriander leaves.

Nutritional Value:

Calories: 187 | Carbohydrate: 32g | Protein: 10g | Sugars: 6g | Fat: 2g | Dietary Fiber: 11g | Cholesterol: 4mg | Sodium: 385mg | Potassium: 934mg

AVIAL (MIXED VEGETABLE) CURRY

Preparation: 15 minutes | Cooking: 20 minutes | Servings: 3

Ingredients:

- Turmeric powder - ½ teaspoon
- Water - 2 to 3 cups
- Mixed vegetables (elephant foot yam, carrot, yellow cucumber, drumstick, potato, chayote) - 2 cups
- Salt - as per taste
- Water – for cooking purpose 2-3 cups

For the Paste:

- Yogurt - ¼ cup
- Grated coconut - ½ cup
- Cumin seeds - ½ teaspoon
- Green chilies - 2 to 3

For Garnishing:

- Coconut oil - 2 teaspoons

- Curry leaves – 10

Cooking Directions:

- Wash the vegetables three – four times.
- Cut the vegetables into 3 inch long pieces.
- Put the vegetables in the Instant Pot.
- Close the lid and also the pressure valve.
- Select pressure cook manual for 4 minutes.
- When the timer beeps, quick release the pressure.
- Add the required amount of salt to the vegetables, once cooked.
- Grind cumin, green chilies, yogurt, and coconut together until it turns into a fine paste.
- Add the paste into the cooked vegetables.
- Set the Instant Pot to SAUTÉ mode high for two minutes and keep stirring.
- In another small pan, heat 1 teaspoon coconut oil on the stovetop.
- When the oil becomes hot add mustard seed to splutter.
- Next add curry leaves in the oil to sizzle.
- Transfer the entire tempering mix on to the avial.
- Pour the remaining 1 teaspoon of raw coconut oil over the avial and stir.
- The avial is ready to serve.

Nutritional Value:

Calories: 665 | Carbohydrate: 70g | Protein: 17g | Sugars: 9g | Fat: 40g | Dietary Fiber: 24g | Cholesterol: 7mg | Sodium: 541mg | Potassium: 1097mg

KADAI MUSHROOM CURRY

Preparation: 10 minutes | Cooking: 20 minutes | Servings: 4

Ingredients:

- Julienned capsicum - 1 large
- Button mushrooms - ½ pound
- Coriander seeds, dry roasted - 1 tablespoon
- Red chilies, roasted - 2 to 3
- Onion, finely chopped - 1 medium
- Garam masala powder - ½ teaspoon
- Ginger garlic paste - 1 teaspoon
- Tomatoes - 3 medium
- Oil - ½ tablespoon
- Kasuri methi (fenugreek leaves) - 1 teaspoon
- Salt – to taste

For Garnishing:

- Coriander leaves - 2 tablespoons

- Ginger juliennes - few

Cooking directions:

- Wash the mushrooms two to three times and cut into small pieces.
- Take the mentioned amounts of tomatoes and puree them using a blender.
- Now grind the roasted coriander and chilies into a fine powder.
- Select cooking mode to SAUTÉ high on the Instant Pot.
- Pour oil when the display appears 'hot.'
- Add the finely chopped onions and sauté for about 4 minutes until the onions turn brown.
- Add ginger garlic paste to the pan and fry it for nearly a minute or until the raw aroma of the paste disappears.
- Now add the grounded coriander-chili mix into the pan.
- Continue stirring and add the tomato puree.
- At this point put in the julienned capsicum and chopped mushrooms.
- Add about ½ to ¾ cups of water.
- Put in the required amount of salt.
- Press START/STOP to cancel sautéing.
- Close the lid and select PRESSURE cook manual high for 2 minutes.
- When the timer beeps release the pressure quickly, use the quick release option.
- Open the lid and add fenugreek powder along with garam masala powder.
- Again select sauté low.
- Stir it for about a minute and then garnish using coriander leaves.
- The Instant Pot mushroom curry is ready to serve.
- Serve hot along with naan or chapatti.

Nutritional Value:

Calories: 59.5 | Carbohydrate: 9.2g | Protein: 3g | Fat: 2.1g | Dietary Fiber: 2.1g | Cholesterol: 0.0mg | Sodium: 103.9mg

NAVARATAN KORMA

Preparation: 40 minutes | Cooking: 30 minutes |
Servings: 5 to 6

Ingredients:

Vegetables:

- Frozen peas or shelled peas - ½ cup
- Peeled and chopped carrots - 2 medium
- Green beans - ¼ cup
- Diced potato - 1 large
- Baby corn - 8 to 9
- Chopped cauliflower - 1 cup

Other Ingredients:

- Green chilies, chopped - 2 to 3
- Onion, thinly sliced - 2 medium
- Fresh curd - ½ cup
- Ginger garlic paste - ½ tablespoon
- Garam masala powder - ¼ teaspoon
- Fresh low-fat cream - ⅓ cup
- Red chili powder - 1 teaspoon
- Turmeric powder - ½ teaspoon
- Water - 1 cup
- Ghee - 2 tablespoons
- Salt – to taste

For Paste:

- Almonds - 10 to 12
- Poppy seeds - 1 tablespoon
- Melon seeds - 1 tablespoon
- Cashews - 10 to 12
- Water - ¼ cup

For Whole Garam Masala:

- Black cardamom - 1
- Green cardamoms - 2 to 3
- Cinnamon - 1 inch
- Cloves - 3
- Mace - 2 single strands
- Bay Leaf - 1

For Garnishing:

- Peeled and blanched almonds - 6 to 7
- Ghee - 1 tablespoon
- Ginger julienne - 2 teaspoons
- Cashew nuts - 10
- Pistachios - 10
- Chopped pineapple - ½ cup
- Raisins - 1 tablespoon
- Walnut halves - 10
- Mint leaves - 1 tablespoon
- Melon seeds - ½ tablespoon
- Saffron strands - a pinch

Cooking Directions:

Preparing the paste:

- Soak all the dry fruits in hot water for about thirty to forty minutes.
- Later on, the outer layer of almonds must be peeled off completely before adding them into a grinder jar.
- Thoroughly drain the other nuts and seeds mixture and then add them into the grinder jar as well.
- Add about ¼ cups of water and grind them until they turn into a smooth fine paste.
- Add more water if required to attain an excellent paste consistency.
- Keep this paste aside.

Cooking the main recipe:

- Place the insert pot in the Instant Pot and set the cooking mode to SAUTÉ high.
- When the display shows 'hot,' add the mentioned amount of ghee and heat for half a minute.
- Once the ghee starts to melt, add whole garam masala and fry it for 1-2 minutes until you hear the crackling sound.
- Add the onions to the pan and sauté for about 3-4 minutes until they turns golden brown.
- Now, add finely chopped green chilies and ginger garlic paste to the pan and sauté for about 2-3 minutes, until the raw aroma disappears.
- At this point add the ground nuts-seeds paste.
- Add mentioned amounts of curd along with the nuts-seeds paste and keep stirring it on low heat for a minute.
- Then, add red chili powder and turmeric to the pan and stir for a minute.
- Add all the vegetables to the pan and stir continuously for three minutes.
- You need to keep stirring to avoid the mixture from sticking at the bottom of the pan.
- Next, add about one cup of water to the pan and season it using salt.
- Now stop sautéing mode by pressing START/STOP.
- Close the lid and also seal the pressure valve.
- Select PRESSURE cook high for 3 minutes.
- When the timer beeps, allow for a natural pressure release.
- After that, again select sauté mode high.
- Stir in cream to the mix of sauce and sauté for a minute.
- Put off the Instant Pot by pressing START/STOP.
- Sprinkle some garam masala powder over the recipe and keep it aside by covering with a lid.

Garnishing the recipe:

- On a stovetop, put a small frying pan and heat about one tablespoon of ghee.
- Add six to seven blanched almonds to the pan and sauté until they turn to a pale golden color.
- Slide these almonds to one side of the pan and add ten cashews, ten pistachios, ten walnut halves and sauté until the cashews turn golden brown.
- Add about one tablespoon of raisins and half a tablespoon of melon seeds to the pan and sauté them for a few seconds.
- Add half a cup of chopped pineapples and sauté it for about a minute.

- Next, add one tablespoon of mint leaves, two teaspoons of julienned ginger and a pinch of kesar (saffron) strands.
- Sauté for a minute under low heat.
- Pour this into the pan of Navaratan korma.
- Serve the Navaratan korma hot with naan, tandoori roti or parathas.

Nutritional Value:

Calories: 275.2 | Carbohydrate: 21.8g | Protein: 5.3g | Sugars: 1.8g | Fat: 20.1g | Dietary Fiber: 4.2g | Cholesterol: 7.4mg

VEGETABLE KORMA

Preparation: 20 minutes | Cooking: 40 minutes | Servings: 4

Ingredients:

For Paste:

- Cashews - 15
- Desiccated coconut - 5 tablespoons
- Roasted chana dal (chickpeas) - ½ tablespoon
- Poppy seeds - 2 teaspoons
- Fennel seeds (saunf) - 1 teaspoon
- Coriander seeds - ½ tablespoon
- Cloves - 3
- Cumin seeds - ½ teaspoon
- Black peppercorns - 4 to 5
- Green cardamoms - 2
- Stone flower - 1
- Capers (Marathi moggu) - 1
- Garlic - 3 to 4 cloves
- Green chilies - 2
- Chopped ginger - ¾ inch
- Water - ½ cup

Vegetables:

- Diced potato - ¾ cup
- Cauliflower florets - ½ cup
- French beans - ¼ cup
- Green peas - ⅓ cup
- Chopped carrots - ½ cup

Other Ingredients:

- Finely chopped onion - ⅓ cup

- Oil - 2 tablespoons
- Curry leaves - 7 to 8
- Diced tomatoes - ⅓ cup
- Red chili powder - ½ teaspoon
- Turmeric powder - ¼ teaspoon
- Water - 1½ cup
- Fresh curd - 2 tablespoons
- Chopped coriander leaves - 2 to 3 tablespoons
- Salt – to taste

Cooking Directions:

Preparing the Veg Korma:

- Soak the cashews in hot water for about twenty to thirty minutes. Later on, drain and keep them aside.
- Rinse the afore mentioned amounts of cauliflower florets and then soak in hot water for about fifteen to twenty minutes. Drain the florets and keep them aside as well.
- Rinse the other vegetables, peel them and chop into small pieces.
- Add all the ingredients mentioned under the paste section into a wet grinder jar.
- Pour in about ½ cup of water and grind them into a fine paste.

Cooking the Korma:

- Select sauté mode high on your Instant Pot.
- Wait for the display to show 'hot,' and pour in two tablespoons of oil.
- Put in the chopped onions and sauté for 3-4 minutes until the onions turn a light brown color.
- Add about seven to eight curry leaves and stir them for a minute.
- Next, add finely chopped tomatoes, ½ a teaspoon of red chili powder and ¼ teaspoon of turmeric powder into the cooker.
- Sauté for two to three minutes.
- Afterwards, add the finely grounded paste into the Instant Pot and stir continuously.
- Reduce the heat setting to low and keep stirring for four to five minutes until the raw aroma of the paste disappears.
- Later on, add two tablespoons of fresh curd and make sure it mixes well with the masala.
- Add all the chopped vegetables and stir for one to two minutes.
- Add one and a half cups of water to make a thin sauce.
- Season the sauce with salt as per your taste.
- Now, it's time to pressure cook the vegetable korma.
- Stop sautéing by pressing START/STOP.
- Close the lid and select pressure cook manual high for 4 minutes.
- When the timer beeps, allow for a natural pressure release.
- Once the pressure gets settled down, open up the lid and check the consistency of the sauce.
- If the sauce is light, then you can simmer the vegetable korma in SAUTÉ mode for a few more minutes, without closing the lid.

- If the sauce looks thick, then you can add a cup of water and simmer it on SAUTÉ mode for a few minutes. (Depending on the thickness of the sauce, you can add water or cook further to maintain the consistency of korma.)
- The texture must be medium and not thin or too thick.
- Once you have attained the desired consistency level, add two to three tablespoons of chopped coriander leaves and stir.
- Serve hot along with chapattis or pooris.

Nutritional Value:

Calories: 279.42 | Carbohydrate: 44.8g | Protein: 15.3g | Sugars: 3.9g | Fat: 9.4g | Dietary Fiber: 8.1g | Cholesterol: 2.5mg

CAULIFLOWER AND POTATO STIR FRY

Cooking: 15 minutes | Servings: 2

Ingredients:
- Cauliflower – 2 cups, cut into florets
- Cubed potato – 1 cup
- Ghee – 1 tbsp.
- Cumin seeds – ½ tsp.
- Green chili pepper – 1, split into two
- Onion – ½, chopped
- Tomato – ½ chopped
- Ginger – 1 tsp. minced
- Garlic – 1 tsp. minced
- Dry mango powder – ½ tsp. or lemon juice
- Cilantro for garnish

Spices:
- Ground turmeric – ¼ tsp.
- Red chili powder – ¼ tsp.
- Coriander powder – ½ tsp.
- Garam masala – ¼ tsp.
- Salt – ½ tsp.

Cooking Directions:
- Press Sauté on your IP and heat oil.
- Add green chili and cumin seeds, sauté for 30 seconds.
- Add garlic paste, ginger, and diced onions. Stir them.
- Add all the spices and chopped tomatoes.
- Add potato cubes and mix.
- Stir fry for 2 minutes.
- Add cauliflower florets and mix.

- Remove any stuck bits from the bottom.
- Add 1/8 cup water and deglaze the pot if necessary.
- Cover and press Manual.
- Cook on Low for 2 minutes.
- Do a natural release.
- Add dry mango powder and garnish with cilantro.
- Serve.

Nutritional Value:

Calories: 153, Fat: 7.83g, Carb: 19.42g, Protein: 4.59g

EGG CURRY

Cooking: 25 minutes | Servings: 2

Ingredients:
- Eggs – 3
- Ghee – 1 tbsp.
- Cumin seeds – ½ tsp.
- Green chili – 1, sliced
- Onion – ¾ cup, chopped
- Ginger – 1 tsp, minced
- Garlic – 1 tsp, minced
- Tomato – ¾ cup, diced
- Water – ½ cup, divided
- Coconut milk – ¼ cup
- Lemon juice – ½ tbsp.
- Cilantro – 1 tbsp. for garnish

Spices:
- Ground turmeric – ¼ tsp.
- Coriander powder – 1 tsp.
- Kashmiri red chili powder – ¼ tsp.
- Garam masala – ¼ tsp.
- Salt – ¼ tsp.
- Whole spices
- Cinnamon – ½ stick
- Bay leaf – 1
- Black peppercorns – ½ tsp.
- Green cardamom – 1

Cooking Directions:
- Press Sauté on your IP.

- Add oil, cumin seeds, and whole spices.
- Add garlic, ginger, onion, and green chili once the cumin changes color.
- Stir fry for 3 minutes.
- Add spices and tomato.
- Stir fry for 2 minutes.
- Add ¼ cup water and deglaze the pot.
- Place the trivet, and a steel bowl with eggs in it.
- Cover with the lid and cook on High for 6 minutes.
- Do a quick release.
- Gently remove the bowl with the eggs. Cool the eggs and peel them.
- With a fork, make holes in the egg surface.
- Add ¼-cup water and coconut milk.
- Add back the peeled eggs in the pot.
- Press Sauté and stir fry for 3 minutes.
- Turn off the IP.
- Add lemon juice and garnish with cilantro.
- Serve.

Nutritional Value:

Calories: 268, Fat: 20g, Carb: 13g, Protein: 10g

Butter Chickpeas

Cooking: 50 minutes | Servings: 2

Ingredients:
- Dried chickpeas – 1 cup, soaked overnight, then drained and rinsed
- Oil – 1 tbsp.
- Onion – ½, diced
- Minced garlic – 1 ½ tsp.
- Minced ginger – ½ tsp.

Spices:
- Garam masala – ½ tsp.
- Coriander powder – ½ tsp.
- Paprika – ½ tsp.
- Salt – ½ tsp.
- Turmeric – ½ tsp.
- Black pepper – to taste
- Cayenne – to taste
- Ground cumin – to taste
- Tomato sauce – 1
- Water – ¾ cup

Add later:
- Green bell pepper – ½, chopped
- Coconut cream – ¼ cup, unsweetened
- Pinch of dried fenugreek leaves
- Cilantro for garnish

Cooking Directions:

- Press the sauté button.
- Add the oil and heat.
- Add the onion and stir fry for 6 to 7 minutes.
- Add the spices, ginger, and garlic and add the tomato sauce, chickpeas, and water.
- Cover with the lid and cook on High for 35 minutes.
- Do a natural pressure release.
- Add fenugreek leaves, cream, and bell pepper. Mix well.
- Garnish with cilantro and serve.

Nutritional Value:

Calories: 470, Fat: 13.3g, Carb: 70.8g, Protein: 21.4g

VEGETABLE BIRYANI

Cooking: 15 minutes | Servings: 2

Ingredients:
- Basmati rice – ½ cup (soaked for 15 minutes, then drained)
- Oil – 1 tbsp.

Whole Spice:
- Cardamom pods – 2
- Whole cloves – 2
- Bay leaf – 1
- Cinnamon stick – ¼
- Cumin seeds – ¼ tsp.
- Fennel seeds – ¼ tsp.
- Onion – ½, thinly sliced
- Minced garlic – 1 tsp.
- Minced ginger – ½ tsp.

Ground spices:
- Salt – ½ tsp.
- Coriander powder – ½ tsp.
- Paprika – ½ tsp.
- Garam masala – to taste
- Black pepper – to taste
- Cayenne – to taste

- Ground cumin - to taste
- Turmeric – to taste

Vegetables:
- Bell pepper – ½, cut into strips
- Baby carrots – ½ cup
- Frozen veggies – ½ cup
- Gold potatoes – ¼ pound, cut in half
- Water – ½ cup
- Cilantro leaves, mint leaves
- Ghee coated cashews and raisins

Cooking Directions:

- Press Sauté and add the oil to the pot.
- Add the whole spice to the hot oil and stir.
- Once the cumin is brown, add the onions, and stir-fry for 5 to 7 minutes.
- Add the ground spices, ginger, garlic, and stir.
- Add the vegetables, rice, and water and stir.
- Cover and cook 6 minutes at High.
- Do a natural release.
- Open and add mint, cilantro, cashews, and raisins.
- Mix and serve.

Nutritional Value:

Calories: 305, Fat: 8.3g, Carb: 52.8g, Protein: 5.9g

VEGETABLE KORMA

Cooking: 20 minutes | Servings: 2

Ingredients:
Onion tomato sauce:

- Onion – ½, roughly chopped
- Garlic – 2 cloves, chopped
- Ginger – 1 inch, chopped
- Tomato -1/2 chopped
- Serrano pepper or green chili – ¼ tsp.

Cashew Sauce:
- Water – ½ cup
- Cashews – ¼ cup
- Heavy cream – 2 tbsps.
- Ghee – 1 ½ tbsps.
- Cashews – 2 tbsps.

- Golden raisins - 2 tbsps.
- Cumin seeds – ¼ tsp.

Spices:

- Paprika – 1 tsp.
- Salt – 1/2 tsp.
- Coriander powder – ½ tsp.
- Turmeric powder – ¼ tsp.
- Garam masala – ¼ tsp.
- Cayenne – a pinch
- Ground cardamom - a pinch
- Chopped potato – 1 cup
- Water – ½ cup
- Chopped vegetables – 2 cups (broccoli, green beans, peas, carrots)
- Dried fenugreek leaves – ¼ tsp.
- Cilantro for garnish

Cooking Directions:

- To make the tomato sauce: in a blender, add the serrano, tomato, ginger, garlic, and onion and blend until smooth. Set aside.
- Prepare the cashew sauce: blend heavy cream, cashews, and water until smooth. Set aside.
- Press the sauté on the Instant Pot.
- Add the ghee, golden raisins and cashews.
- Stir fry until the cashews turn golden.
- Remove the raisins and cashews from the pot and set aside.
- Add the cumin seeds to the pot.
- Once they start to brown, add the tomato and onion mixture.
- Stir fry for 7 to 8 minutes.
- Add all the remaining spices and the potatoes. Mix well.
- Add the water and cover.
- Cook on High for 5 minutes.
- Do a quick release.
- Add the remaining chopped vegetables.
- Cover and cook on High for 2 minutes.
- Do a quick release.
- Stir in fenugreek leaves, and cashew sauce.
- Garnish with ghee-coated raisins, and cashews and cilantro.
- Serve.

Nutritional Value:

Calories: 380, Fat: 24.6g, Carb: 31.1g, Protein: 8.6g

Spiced Potato and Eggplant

Cooking: 5 minutes | Servings: 2

Ingredients:

- Oil – ½ tbsp.
- Cumin seeds – ¼ tsp.
- Serrano pepper – ½, minced
- Golden potatoes – ½ pound, chopped
- Eggplant – ¾ pound, chopped
- Water – ¼ cup
- Onion masala – ¼ cup (recipe below)
- Salt – ½ tsp.
- Garam masala – ¼ tsp.
- Cilantro for garnish

Cooking Directions:

- Press the Sauté and add oil.
- Add serrano pepper and cumin seeds to the hot oil.
- Add the remaining ingredients once the cumin seeds are brown.
- Cover with the lid and cook on High for 4 minutes.
- Do a quick release.
- Mix well.
- Garnish and serve.

Nutritional Value:

Calories: 155, Fat: 3.8g, Carb: 29.5g, Protein: 3.4g

Langar Dal

Cooking: 30 minutes | Servings: 2

Ingredients:

- Ghee – 2 tbsps. divided
- Cumin seeds – ½ tsp.
- Urad dal – ½ cup, soaked in cold water overnight
- Chana dal – 2 tbsp.
- Water – 2 cups
- Onion masala – ½ cup
- Salt – ¾ tsp.
- Garam masala – ¾ tsp.
- Cayenne – ¼ tsp.
- Cilantro and heavy cream for garnish

Cooking Directions:

- Press the sauté button on the IP.
- Add 1 tbsp. ghee to the pot and add cumin seeds to the melted ghee.
- Add the remaining ingredients to the pot when the cumin seeds are brown.
- Cover and cook on High for 30 minutes.
- Do a natural release.
- Stir in the remaining ingredients.
- Garnish with the cilantro and heavy cream and serve.

Nutritional Value:

Calories: 338, Fat: 13.6g, Carb: 39.1g, Protein: 16g

EGG BIRYANI

Cooking: 20 minutes | Servings: 2

Ingredients:

- Basmati rice – 1 cup, soaked for 15 minutes
- Ghee – 2 tbsps.

Whole spices:

- Cardamom pods – 5
- Whole cloves – 4
- Bay leaf – 2
- Cinnamon stick – ½ inch
- Cumin seeds – ½ tsp.
- Fennel seeds – ½ tsp.
- Oil – 2 tbsps.
- Onion – 1, thinly sliced
- Minced garlic – 2 tsps.
- Minced ginger – 1 tsp.
- Tomato – 1, diced

Ground spices:

- Salt – 1 ½ tsp.
- Coriander powder – 1 tsp.
- Paprika – 1 tsp.
- Garam masala – ½ tsp.
- Black pepper – ¼ tsp.
- Cayenne – ¼ tsp.
- Ground cumin – ¼ tsp.
- Turmeric – ¼ tsp.
- Water – 1 cup
- Eggs – 6

- Cilantro leaves, chopped
- Mint leaves, chopped
- Ghee coated raisins and cashews

Cooking Directions:

- Press the sauté button and add the oil to the Instant Pot.
- Add the whole spices and stir.
- Add the onions once the cumin seeds are brown.
- Stir-fry for 5 to 7 minutes.
- Add the ground spices, ginger, garlic, and tomato.
- Cook for 2 to 3 minutes.
- Add the rice and water.
- Then place a steamer basket on top of the rice.
- Place the eggs in the steamer basket.
- Cover and cook on High for 10 minutes.
- Do a quick release.
- Remove the eggs, cool and peel them. You can stir fry the eggs if necessary.
- Place the peeled eggs back into the rice and mix well.
- Garnish with ghee coated cashews and raisins, mint, and cilantro.
- Serve.

Nutritional Value:

Calories: 835, Fat: 41.9g, Carb: 91.4g, Protein: 25.7g

Indian Desserts

Gulab Jamun

Preparation: 30 - 35 minutes | Cooking: 15 minutes | Servings: 8

Ingredients:

- Milk (full-fat milk) - 6 tablespoon
- Bread - 8 pieces
- Water - $1/5$ cup
- Sugar - 1 cup
- Almonds, sliced - 4
- Cardamom powder - 1 teaspoon
- Raisins - 8
- Oil - 5 cups
- Chopped almonds - ¼ cup

Cooking Directions:

- Take a pan and add sugar and water to it.
- On a stovetop, set to medium heat and keep stirring to form a sugar syrup.
- Once the sugar gets dissolved, and forms into a syrup consistency spread green cardamom powder over it.
- Take the bread on a separate plate and cut and remove the crusts. Then cut the remaining bread into small pieces.
- Pour the mentioned quantity of milk all over the pieces and make it into a dough.
- You need to add milk slowly to create a dough-like texture with the bread.
- Now with the bread dough, make small rounded balls.
- Flatten the dough and put almonds and raisins in and again make it a ball.
- Set the Instant Pot to SAUTÉ low.
- When the display shows 'hot,' pour in oil and wait for it to sizzle.
- Add the rounded ball dough to the oil and fry it.
- When the dough ball becomes slightly brown increase the temperature to high and continue with the frying process, until it becomes golden brown.
- Press START/STOP for stopping the sautéing.
- Now remove it from the pan.
- Put it directly into the Gulab Jamun syrup already prepared.
- Keep the Gulab Jamun on low heat for about 5 minutes.
- The more the Gulab Jamun rest on the sugar syrup, it will have a better taste.
- Garnish the Gulab Jamun with dry fruits.

Nutritional Value:

Calories: 230 | Carbohydrate: 40g | Protein: 3g | Sugars: 28g | Fat: 7g | Dietary Fiber: 1g | Cholesterol: 1mg | Sodium: 175mg | Potassium: 72mg

INSTANT POT GAJAR HALWA

Preparation: 15 minutes | Cooking: 30 minutes | Servings: 3

Ingredients:

- Milk - 2½ cups
- Grated carrots - 2¼ pounds
- Sugar - 8 tablespoons
- Chopped cashews - 8 to 10
- Chopped almonds – 8-10
- Pistachios, chopped - 7 to 8
- Cardamom powder – ½ teaspoon
- Saffron – a pinch
- Ghee/oil - 3 to 4 tablespoons

Cooking Directions:

1. Prepare the carrots after washing thoroughly.
2. Peel the skin and grate the carrots.
3. Set your Instant Pot to SAUTÉ mode high.
4. Wait for the 'hot' display to appear, pour in ghee and the carrot.
5. Cook for about 3 minutes by covering the lid.
6. Press START/STOP to cease sautéing.
7. Now add milk, close the lid and vent.
8. Select PRESSURE COOK manual high for 5 minutes.
9. After hearing the beeping, do a quick pressure release.
10. Open the lid and add cardamom, sugar, cashews, almonds, pistachios, saffron and raisins.
11. Mix in all the ingredients.
12. Select SAUTÉ mode high and cook for 6-7 minutes until the gajar halwa thickens.
13. Keep stirring the mixture until it turns dry.
14. Now add the dry fruits and cook for about 5 minutes.
15. Serve cold.

Nutritional Value:

Calories: 188 | Carbohydrate: 32g | Protein: 5g | Sugars: 27g | Fat: 8g | Dietary Fiber: 2g | Cholesterol: 5mg | Sodium: 158mg | Potassium: 450mg

SWEET PONGAL

Preparation: 5 minutes | Cooking: 25 minutes | Servings: 5

Ingredients:

- Yellow moong dal (split yellow gram) - ¼ cup
- Rice - ½ cup
- Ghee - 2 tablespoons
- Chopped jaggery - 1 cup
- Nutmeg - a pinch
- Cardamom powder - ½ teaspoon
- Raisins - 2 tablespoons
- Broken cashew nuts - 2 tablespoons
- Water - 3¼ cups

Cooking directions:

1. Set Instant Pot to SAUTE mode high.
2. Put the yellow moong dal and rice into it when the display shows 'hot.'
3. Sauté it for about four minutes.
4. Press START/STOP and cancel the sautéing.
5. After cooling the roasted ingredients, wash the dried items and strain it.
6. Put the strained yellow moong dal-rice mixture along with three cups of water in the Instant Pot.
7. Close the lid and pressure valve.
8. Now select RICE mode on the Instant Pot.
9. When the timer beeps, allow it to release the pressure naturally.
10. Once the pressure has settled down, open up the lid and mash the dal and rice using a spoon. Keep it aside.
11. Now on the stovetop place a non-stick pan and heat about ¼ cups of water in it.
12. Add one tablespoon of ghee and jaggery to the pan and cook it on medium heat for about two minutes.
13. Keep stirring the mixture continuously.
14. Add the yellow moong dal and rice mixture to the pan, along with nutmeg powder and cardamom powder.
15. Mix them and cook it on medium temperature for two to three minutes.
16. Keep them aside.
17. Put another nonstick pan on stovetop and heat on medium temperature.
18. When the pan becomes hot add one tablespoon of ghee.
19. Sauté raisins and cashews in it for two minutes.
20. Add these fried cashews and raisins to the prepared mix, and the Sweet Pongal is ready to serve.

Nutritional Value:

Calories: 272 | Carbohydrate: 48.7g | Protein: 3.8g | Fat: 6.9g | Dietary Fiber: 1.4g | Cholesterol: 0mg | Sodium: 2.1mg

KAJU BARFI

Preparation: 15 minutes | Cooking: 10 minutes | Servings: 20

Ingredients:

- Sugar - ½ cup
- Water - ½ cup
- Cashew nuts, broken - 1 cup
- Ghee - 2 tablespoons
- Cardamom powder - ½ teaspoon

Cooking Directions:

1. Prepare the cashew nuts by blending in a mixer.
2. On your Instant Pot, select sauté mode high.
3. Add sugar and water to the pan. Sauté for about three minutes.
4. Keep stirring it.
5. Once the sugar forms to syrup consistency, add the blended cashew powder into it.
6. Mix it well together and cook it on medium temperature for two minutes, by continuously stirring it.
7. Afterward, add cardamom powder and mix well for about 2 minutes.
8. Press START/STOP to cancel sautéing.
9. Take a plate and spread melted ghee.
10. Transfer the mixture to the plate and spread evenly.
11. Let the mixture cool for about two to three minutes.
12. Once the heat settled down, cut it into eight equal diamond size pieces.
13. Serve hot or cold.

Nutritional Value:

Calories: 48 | Carbohydrate: 5.7g | Protein: 1.1g | Fat: 2.3g | Dietary Fiber: 0.1g | Cholesterol: 0mg | Sodium: 0.6mg

PAAL **P**AYASAM **(S**OUTH **I**NDIAN **D**ESSERT IN **M**ILK**)**

Preparation: 5 minutes | Cooking: 13 minutes | Servings: 4

Ingredients:

- Long grained rice (basmati) - ¼ cup
- Full fat milk - 4½ cups
- Saffron - ¼ teaspoon
- Warm full-fat milk - ¼ cup
- Cardamom powder - ½ teaspoon
- Sugar - ½ cup

Cooking Directions:

1. The long-grained rice must be soaked in water for about thirty minutes and then drained. Keep this aside.
2. On your Instant Pot, select SAUTÉ mode low.

3. When the display shows 'hot,' add milk and warm for about 3-4 minutes.
4. Combine saffron to the milk.
5. Press STOP/START to stop sautéing.
6. Put the drained rice to the Instant Pot with saffron mixed milk.
7. Add sugar and cardamom powder.
8. Stir all the ingredients.
9. Close the lid and seal the pressure vent.
10. Select PORRIDGE mode high pressure for 20 minutes.
11. When the timer beeps, go for a quick pressure release.
12. Open the lid and mix the dessert.
13. Serve hot or cold.

Nutritional Value:

Calories: 408 | Carbohydrate: 43.4g | Protein: 10.9g | Fat: 15.5g | Dietary Fiber: 0.4g | Cholesterol: 38mg | Sodium: 45.7mg

SOUP RECIPES

TOMATO SOUP

Preparation: 25 minutes | Cooking: 20 minutes | Servings: 4

Ingredients:

- Finely chopped onion - 1 small
- Tomato - 4 large
- Bay Leaf - 1
- Garlic cloves - 2 to 3
- Butter - 1 tablespoon
- Corn starch (corn flour + water) - 1 teaspoon
- Water - 1 cup
- Sugar - ½ tablespoon
- Cream - 1 tablespoon
- Powdered black pepper - as per taste required
- Bread - 1 or 2 slices
- Salt – to taste
- Water – 6 cups

Cooking Directions:

Preparing tomato puree:

- Wash tomatoes and remove the stems.
- Select SAUTÉ high on your Instant Pot.
- After seeing 'hot' display add about 6 cups of water.
- Add a teaspoon of salt and bring to boil.
- Once the water starts to boil add the tomatoes.
- Press START/STOP to cancel sautéing.
- Close the pot using a lid.
- Let the tomatoes stay in hot water for about twenty to thirty minutes
- Later on, drain the water and let the tomatoes cool down.
- During this waiting period, you can finely chop the garlic and onions and keep it aside.
- Once the tomatoes cool down, peel the outer part and slice down the eye part as well.
- Add the tomatoes to a blender jar and blend them until the tomatoes turn into a thick texture.
- Keep this thick and smooth puree aside.

Bread toasting:

- Bread can toast using a frying pan.
- For that select SAUTÉ mode low on your Instant Pot.

- Place bread when you see the 'hot' display.
- Toast the bread for about 1 minute by flipping until it turns brown or becomes crisp on both sides.
- Press START/STOP to cancel sautéing.
- Once the bread is toasted, slice the toast into strips for easy dipping.

Making tomato soup:

- Take about one teaspoon of cornflour and mix it well with two tablespoons of water to bring a smooth paste of cornstarch.
- Now on your Instant Pot, select SAUTÉ mode low.
- Put in 1 tablespoon of butter when 'hot' appears on the display.
- When the butter starts to melt, add a bay leaf and sauté for 1 minute.
- Later on, add finely chopped garlic to the pan and sauté 1 or 2 minutes.
- Add finely chopped onions to the pan and sauté for 3-4 minutes until it turns translucent.
- After a few seconds, add the blended tomato puree to the pot.
- Keep stirring the puree for a minute and then add water, pepper, and salt.
- Keep the temperature on a low heat for about 5-8 minutes and wait until the soup reaches a boiling stage.
- Add the prepared cornflour paste to the soup.
- Stir it well together and simmer the soup for about three to four minutes or until the soup attains a thick texture.
- Add sugar to the soup and stir.
- Now, add 1 tablespoon of cream into the soup and simmer it for a minute.
- Turn off the heat and pour the hot tomato soup into a soup bowl.
- Put the toasted bread pieces into the soup.
- Garnish the tomato soup with coriander leaves.
- The soup is ready to serve.

Nutritional Value:

Calories: 72.6 | Carbohydrate: 61.3g | Protein: 1.9g | Sugars: 9.8g | Fat: 0.7g | Dietary Fiber: 1.5g | Cholesterol: 0.0mg | Sodium: 667mg | Potassium: 277mg

BEETROOT CARROT GINGER SOUP

Preparation: 10 minutes | Cooking: 60 minutes | Servings: 4

Ingredients:

- Olive oil - 1 tablespoon
- Beetroot - 1 pound
- Carrots, coarsely chopped - 1 pound
- Finely chopped onion - 1 cup
- Ginger, fresh, minced - 1 tablespoon
- Water - 6 cups

- Minced garlic - 1 large clove
- Sour cream - 4 teaspoons
- Orange rind - 1 teaspoon
- Ground black pepper - as per taste required
- Salt - if required

Preparing Directions:

- Wash and peel the outer layers of beetroots and chop into large chunks.
- Discard the greens.
- On your Instant Pot, select SAUTÉ mode high.
- When the display illuminates 'hot,' add olive oil.
- Now stir in chopped onions until it turns light brown for 2 minutes.
- Add ginger, carrots, and garlic to the skillet and sauté for 2 minutes.
- Press STOP/START to cease sautéing.
- Add water and diced beetroots to the Instant Pot.
- Add orange rind to the soup and continue stirring.
- Cover the Instant Pot and also seal the pressure vent.
- Select PRESSURE COOK high for 5 minutes.
- After the beep, quick release the pressure.
- Transfer the mix to a blender and puree the soup.
- Taste the soup and add seasoning as per your taste required.
- If you prefer salt, add some salt.
- Garnish with sour cream.
- The soup is ready to serve hot.

Nutritional Value:

Calories: 141 | Carbohydrate: 25g | Protein: 2.4g |Fat: 3.8g | Dietary Fiber: 6.2g | Cholesterol: 0.0mg | Sodium: 1608.9mg

MUTTON SHORBA

Preparation: 10 minutes | Cooking: 40 minutes | Servings: 5

Ingredients:

- Mutton ribs - ½ pound
- Finely chopped onion - 1 large
- Cloves - 5
- Cinnamon stick - 1 inch
- Pepper powder - 1 tablespoon
- Ginger – 1 tablespoon
- Garlic paste – 1 tablespoon
- Red chili powder - 1 teaspoon

- Cumin powder - 1 teaspoon
- Oil - 2 tablespoons
- Finely chopped mint leaves - ¼ cup
- Finely chopped coriander leaves - ½ cup
- Lemon - 2 slices
- Salt - as per taste
- Water – 4 cups

Preparing Directions:

1. Set cooking to SAUTÉ mode high on your Instant Pot.
2. When the display 'hot' illuminates, add oil and chopped onions.
3. Sauté it for a minute or until the onions turn light brown.
4. Now, add cumin, pepper, and red chili powders to the pan and sauté them for a minute.
5. Add ginger, and garlic paste along with a pinch of turmeric powder. Sauté for 3 minutes.
6. Afterward, add crushed cinnamon, and cloves and continue sautéing.
7. Pour 4 cups of water and mutton.
8. Add salt as required and stir the soup.
9. Press START/STOP for canceling the sauté mode.
10. Close the lid and pressure valve.
11. Select SOUP mode high pressure.
12. When the alarm beeps allow natural pressure release.
13. Open the lid and carefully transfer the mutton to a plate.
14. After cooling remove the meat from the bone and put it back to the cooker.
15. Add coriander leaves, mint and select SAUTÉ low for 5 minutes.
16. Press START/STOP to cancel sautéing.
17. Your soup is ready to serve.

Nutritional Value:

Calories: 274 | Carbohydrate: 10g | Protein: 27g | Sugars: 0g | Fat: 14g | Dietary Fiber: 0g | Cholesterol: 0.0mg | Sodium: 1705mg | Potassium: 0mg

INSTANT POT LENTIL SOUP

Preparation: 10 minutes | Cooking: 25 minutes | Servings: 4

Ingredients:

For Moong Dal Puree:

- Chopped onions - ½ cup
- Carrot - ¼ cup
- Yellow moong dal - 3 tablespoons

Other Ingredients:

- Oil - 2 teaspoon

- Corn flour - ½ tablespoon
- Chopped garlic - ½ teaspoon
- Chopped onions - ½ cup
- Cooked barley - 2 tablespoons
- Chopped celery - 2 tablespoons
- Salt – as required
- Water – 2¼ cups

Preparing Directions:

For Moong Dal Puree:

- Wash the moong dal and then soak it in water for about two to three hours.
- Afterwards, drain the water from the moong dal and combine it with carrots and onions in an Instant Pot Cooker.
- Add two cups of water to the cooker.
- Close the lid and seal the pressure valve.
- Set pressure cooking manual high mode for 15 minutes.
- After beeping allow it cool naturally for 10-15 minutes.
- Wait until the steam escapes and then open the pressure cooker.
- Allow the cooked dal mix to cool and then blend it using a mixer to form a fine puree.

Preparing the soup:

1. Take cornflour and mix it with ¼ cup of water in a separate bowl.
2. Now, set your Instant Pot to sauté high.
3. When 'hot' appears on the display add garlic, onions, and celery to the pan and sauté it on medium temperature for a minute.
4. Later on, add the dal puree to the pan and mix it well.
5. Change the sauté mode to low and let the soup cook on low heat for about 2-3 minutes until it boils.
6. Keep stirring the soup occasionally to avoid lumps forming.
7. Add salt, barley, previously mixed cornflour mixture, and pepper to the soup.
8. Mix them well and cook it under low heat for 5 minutes till it simmers.
9. Press start/stop to cease sautéing.
10. The soup is ready to serve hot.

Nutritional Value:

Calories: 106 | Carbohydrate: 16.2g | Protein: 3.9g | Fat: 2.8g | Dietary Fiber: 1.7g | Cholesterol: 0.0mg | Sodium: 5.5mg

CURRIED CHICKEN SOUP

Preparation: 10 minutes | Cooking: 30 minutes | Servings: 4

Ingredients:

- Chicken breast - ½ pound
- Garlic - 1 clove
- Finely diced onion - 1 large
- Finely diced ginger - 2 inches
- Canola oil - 2 tablespoons
- Curry powder - 1 teaspoon
- Cayenne pepper – 1 teaspoon
- Cloves - 2
- Chicken stock - 2½ cup
- Whipping cream - ½ cup
- Cornstarch - 2 teaspoons
- Red lentils - ½ cup
- Cilantro - as required for garnishing
- Black sesame seeds – ¾ teaspoon

Preparing Directions:

- In your Instant Pot, select sauté mode low.
- Wait for 'hot' to appear on the display and add some oil to heat it.
- Sauté the diced vegetables for 3-4 minutes.
- Add chicken to the pan and sauté it for about two to three minutes.
- Sauté with cayenne pepper, salt, cloves, and curry powder for 2-3 minutes.
- Stir in the cream for 3 minutes.
- After that, pour the stock into the pan.
- Bring to boiling and then slow the temperature and simmer for about fifteen minutes.
- For improving the consistency of the soup, add cornstarch.
- Press start/stop for canceling the sauté mode.
- Splutter sesame seeds in a little oil in a pan and spread over the soup for tempering.
- Garnish with cilantro.
- Serve hot.

Nutritional Value:

Calories: 390 | Carbohydrate: 29g | Protein: 25g | Fat: 20g | Dietary Fiber: 10g | Sodium: 300mg

KETO INDIAN RECIPES

KETO MUTTON MASALA

Preparation: 2 hours | Cooking: 50 minutes | Servings: 4

Ingredients:

For Marinating:

- Mutton with bones – 1 pound
- Chili powder – 1 teaspoon
- Turmeric powder – 1 teaspoon
- Yogurt – 3 tablespoons
- Salt: to taste

For Ghee Roast:

- Onion, finely sliced – 1 small
- Coriander powder – 1 teaspoon
- Ghee – 3 tablespoon
- Cumin powder – 1 teaspoon
- Cloves – 3 or 4 pods
- Cinnamon – 1 stick
- Black cardamom – 2 pods
- Bay leaves – 1
- Ginger garlic paste – 1 tablespoon
- Tomatoes (pulped to paste) – 2
- Garam masala powder – 1 teaspoon
- Peppercorns – 4 or 5
- Water – 1¼ cups

Cooking directions:

For Marinating:

- Put the mutton in a bowl and add the marinade mix.
- Rub the mix thoroughly with the mutton and refrigerate for two hours for better argination.

For Ghee Roast:

- In the Instant Pot, select sauté mode high and wait for half second for 'hot' to appear on the display.
- Add ghee to melt and add spices.
- Sauté it for 2-3 minutes until it starts to produce the aroma.

- Turn the heat to low and add onion and keep stirring them slowly for about 3-4 minutes, until they turn soft.
- Add the mentioned amount of ginger garlic paste and cook it together for about two to three minutes. Stir continuously; otherwise, it will stick in the cooker.
- Later on, add the mutton that has been marinated previously to the Instant Pot and roast it for about five minutes until the meat changes its color
- When the mutton changes its color, add cumin, garam masala, and coriander powder. Mix them well and cook for about five minutes. Stir continuously.
- Add tomatoes as a pulp (cut two small tomatoes and grind them to make a paste). Mix them well for five minutes. (Alternatively, you can mash the tomatoes in the cooker. When the tomatoes become soft after cooking, you can mash them with a spoon/spatula)
- Press start/stop to cancel sautéing.
- Add water until the mutton gets thoroughly covered.
- Close the Instant Pot lid and seal the pressure vent.
- Set pressure cook high manual mode for 25 minutes.
- After hearing the timer beep, allow it to do a natural pressure release. It will take about 10-20 minutes.
- Open the cooker and garnish the mutton with finely chopped coriander leaves.
- Serve hot. Ideal to serve with nan/bread or rice.

Nutritional Value:

Calories: 330 | Carbohydrate: 8g | Protein: 28.7g | Sugars: 3.9g | Fat: 330g | Cholesterol: 80mg | Sodium: 1285mg |Dietary fiber: 1.8g

KETO INSTANT POT PANEER BHURJI

Preparation: 5 minutes | Cooking: 25 minutes | Servings: 3

Ingredients:

- Cottage cheese or Paneer - ½ pound
- Butter or Ghee - 2 tablespoons
- Coriander powder - 1 teaspoon
- Turmeric, grounded - ½ teaspoon
- Tomato - ½ cup
- Onion (finely sliced) - ½ cup
- Capsicum or Green Pepper (julienned) – 2
- Ginger, fresh, finely chopped - ½ tablespoon
- Cheddar cheese - 1¾ ounce
- Finely chopped garlic - ½ tablespoon
- Chili (julienned) - 1
- Cumin seeds - 1 teaspoon
- Kashmiri red chili powder - ½ teaspoon
- Salt - as per taste required

- Fresh coriander leaves (chopped) - for seasoning

Cooking Directions:

- In a medium bowl, grate the paneer.
- Select sauté mode in your Instant Pot.
- Wait for the display to appear as 'hot.'
- Add butter/ghee when the pan becomes hot.
- Now, add the sliced onion and sauté it for 4-5 minutes until it becomes translucent.
- Add cumin seeds to the pan and keep stirring for two minutes.
- Add garlic, ginger and green chili and fry them all together for 1 minute until the fragrance emanates.
- Now add chili powder, turmeric and coriander powder and stir continuously for 2-3 minutes.
- When the spices become dry and roasted, add the chopped tomatoes.
- Cover up the pan and let it cook on a low heat for about five to six minutes. Don't forget to stir occasionally.
- Add the paneer, green pepper and salt to the pan
- Add cheese and let it cook for about three to four minutes
- Finally, add fresh coriander and one tablespoon of butter to the pan. Sauté for 2 minutes.
- Stop/Cancel sauté to cease cooking.
- Stir them well and serve it hot.

Nutritional Value:

Calories: 463 | Carbohydrate: 4g | Protein: 22g |Fat: 39g | Fiber: 1g

SPICED MUSTARD GREENS

Preparation: 5 minutes | Cooking: 15 minutes | Servings: 6

Ingredients:

Greens:

- Finely chopped Mustard green leaves - 6 cups
- Finely chopped spinach - 4 cups
- Green chilies, chopped – 2

For Masala Seasoning:

- Coarsely chopped onion - 1 medium
- Butter or ghee - 2 teaspoons
- Ginger garlic paste - 2 tablespoons
- Turmeric powder - ½ teaspoon
- Coriander powder - 3 teaspoons
- Garam masala - 1 teaspoon
- Red chili powder - ½ teaspoon

- Cumin seeds - 1 teaspoon
- Water - ¾ cups
- Corn flour - 2 tablespoons
- Salt - 1 teaspoon or as per taste required

Cooking Directions:

For preparing the greens:

- Rinse and wash spinach leaves and mustard greens to remove any dirt.
- Afterward, remove the stems from the mustard greens and spinach.
- Finely chop it and keep ready to cook.
- Add chopped green chilies.
- Now microwave them together for about two minutes.
- Take a hand blender and puree the greens to an excellent consistency as required.

For preparing the masala:

- Set Instant Pot to sauté mode.
- When the display shows 'hot,' add ginger garlic paste to the pot and sauté it for about thirty seconds.
- Later on, add coarsely chopped onions and sauté them for thirty seconds.
- Finally, add spices, salt, and water.
- Stir them well together and then press the SAUTE button again to cancel the operation.
- Close the lid and set the valve to a sealing position
- Set pressure cook manual high for about two minutes.
- After two minutes, quick release the pressure.
- Open up the lid after the pressure has released completely.
- Turn on the SAUTE button.
- Add finely ground cornmeal and sauté it for about one minute.
- Add a little amount of water as per the required consistency.
- Add pureed greens and sauté them for about two minutes
- Once the flavors set together, the recipe is ready to serve.
- Serve hot with nan or bread.

Nutritional Values:

Calories: 61 | Carbohydrate: 8g | Protein: 2g | Sugars: 2g | Fat: 2g | Cholesterol: 4mg | Sodium: 472mg | Fiber: 3g |Potassium: 365mg |Fiber: 3g

KETO INDIAN LAMB CURRY

Preparation: 15 minutes | Cooking: 1 hour 20 minutes | Servings: 14

Ingredients:

For Marination:

- Olive oil - 2 tablespoons
- Coriander powder - 2 teaspoons
- Turmeric ground - 1 teaspoon
- Finely chopped ginger - 2 teaspoons
- Cumin powder - 2 teaspoons
- Crush garlic - 3 cloves
- Onion powder - 1 teaspoon
- Cardamom fine powder - 1 teaspoon
- Paprika ground - 1 teaspoon
- Kashmiri chili powder - 1 teaspoon

For Curry:

- Lamb shoulder (chopped) - 4 pounds
- Ghee - 3 tablespoons
- Diced onion - 1 medium
- Heavy cream - 1 cup
- Cinnamon ground - 1 teaspoon
- Kashmiri chili powder - 1 teaspoon
- Pepper - 1 teaspoon
- Flaked almonds - 1/2 cup
- Roughly chopped cilantro - 3 tablespoons
- Salt – to taste

Cooking Directions:

For Marination:

- Put all marinade ingredients in a medium size bowl and mix them well.
- Add chopped lamb to the ingredients and mix them.
- Keep the marinated lamb in a fridge for about one hour. The marination can also be refrigerated overnight. If you can marinate for a longer time, it will give a better marinade effect.

For Curry:

- Select sauté mode high on your Instant Pot.
- When the display turns 'hot,' add ghee.
- Once the ghee completely melts down, add cinnamon, onion and chili powder. Sauté it for about 2-3 minutes.
- Add marinated lamb, pepper, and salt and stir them all together.
- Stop sautéing.
- Close the lid and pressure vent of the Instant Pot.
- Select manual pressure cook for 20 minutes.
- When the timer beeps, allow it to release the pressure naturally.
- Open the lid and add heavy cream.

- Sauté it without the lid for about 6 minutes.
- Add flaked almonds and stir them well with the sauce.
- Garnish the curry with coriander leaves.
- Serve hot.

Nutritional Values:

Calories: 480 | Carbohydrate: 2g | Protein: 30g | Sugars: 0.2g | Fat: 38g | Cholesterol: 150mg | Sodium: 586mg | Fiber: 1g | Potassium: 380mg

KETO INDIAN BUTTER CHICKEN

Preparation: 25 minutes | Cooking: 35 minutes | Servings: 4

Ingredients:

For Spice Mixing:

- Black pepper ground - ¼ teaspoon
- Mix garam masala powder - 1½ tablespoons
- Cumin ground - 1 teaspoon
- Coriander powder - ½ teaspoon
- Turmeric - 1/2 teaspoon
- Fenugreek - ¼ teaspoon
- Cinnamon - ¼ teaspoon

For Chicken Marination:

- Chicken breast, boneless and skinless – 1 pound
- Spice mix powder - ¾ (Use from the 2 tablespoons)
- Fresh lemon juice - 2 tablespoons
- Crushed garlic - 2 large cloves
- Sour cream - 3 tablespoons
- Salt: ½ teaspoon

For Sauce:

- Butter - 4 tablespoons
- Diced onion - 1 medium
- Grated fresh ginger - 1 inch
- Crushed garlic - 3 large
- Crushed red pepper flakes - ¼ teaspoon
- Chicken bone broth - 1½ cup
- Tomato paste - 4 tablespoons
- Remaining spice mix - ¾ tablespoon
- Whipping cream - ½ cup
- Salt - ½ teaspoon

For Serving:

- Sliced red onions – For garnishing
- Cilantro leaves – Few as required

Cooking Directions:

- In a medium bowl mix all the spice powders and keep ready.
- In another large bowl, mix all the ingredients mentioned under the chicken section with the chicken.
- Cover them up and refrigerate for about two hours. For a better marinade effect, refrigerate for a more extended period.

Preparing the sauce:

- In your Instant Pot select sauté mode high.
- When the display shows 'hot,' add ghee and onion.
- Keep stirring for about 3 minutes until the onion turns brown
- Stir in ginger, garlic and the ¾ tablespoon spice mix to the insert pan and continue sautéing for about one minute.
- Later on, add crushed red pepper flakes, salt, and tomato paste. Continue stirring for 2 minutes.
- Now add chicken broth.
- Bring them all to a boiling state and then reduce the heat to simmer.
- Let it cook for about ten minutes.
- After that turn off the Instant Pot.
- Now put the marinated chicken into the insert pot. Close the lid and pressure vent.
- Select poultry mode default setting and press start. The default setting is 15 minutes.
- After cooking release the pressure using the quick release option.
- Remove the chicken into a bowl.
- Once the sauce has cooled down, blend the sauce with butter and whipping cream with an immersion blender.
- After combining add back the chicken to the sauce.
- The chicken is ready to serve.
- Garnish with fresh cilantro leaves and sliced red onions.
- Serve hot.

Nutritional Values:

Calories: 469 | Carbohydrate: 9.8g | Protein: 37.7g | Fat: 31g | Sodium: 676mg | Fiber: 1.7g | Potassium: 583mg

CONCLUSION

This book contains the best Indian recipes which are enhanced with unique Indian spices. These flavorsome dishes will make your inner soul satisfied and happy. Not only does the book have best Indian vegetarian and non-vegetarian recipes but it also contains recipes of Indian desserts.

The book will make you feel like saying the expression, 'Small Package Big Explosion (Dhamaka)'. Indian desserts are undoubtedly very delectable and scrumptious. Indian cuisine has the blend of flavorful spices, and the mixture turns out to be the best amongst all.

The best part about Indian Cuisine is that there is always something extra with the average meal. Pickles and chutney are something which is one of the most famous side dishes or extra accompaniments with meals. The contemporary dishes are all about flavors and essence of the spices used in the recipes.

Making food simply and concisely is what Indian Cuisine is about. You simply cannot miss this book which has the best Indian recipes.

With utmost thankfulness and acknowledgment, I thank you and appreciate you from my inner soul for giving your precious time and attendance to this book. Your expression of liking the recipes of this book will always motivate me to explore more on Indian cuisine.

Printed in Great Britain
by Amazon